SIMPLE KALEIDOSCOPES

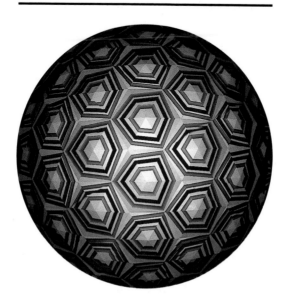

Simple
Kaleidoscopes

24 Spectacular Scopes to Make

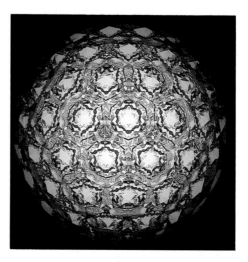

Gary Newlin

Sterling Publishing Co., Inc.   New York
A STERLING/LARK BOOK

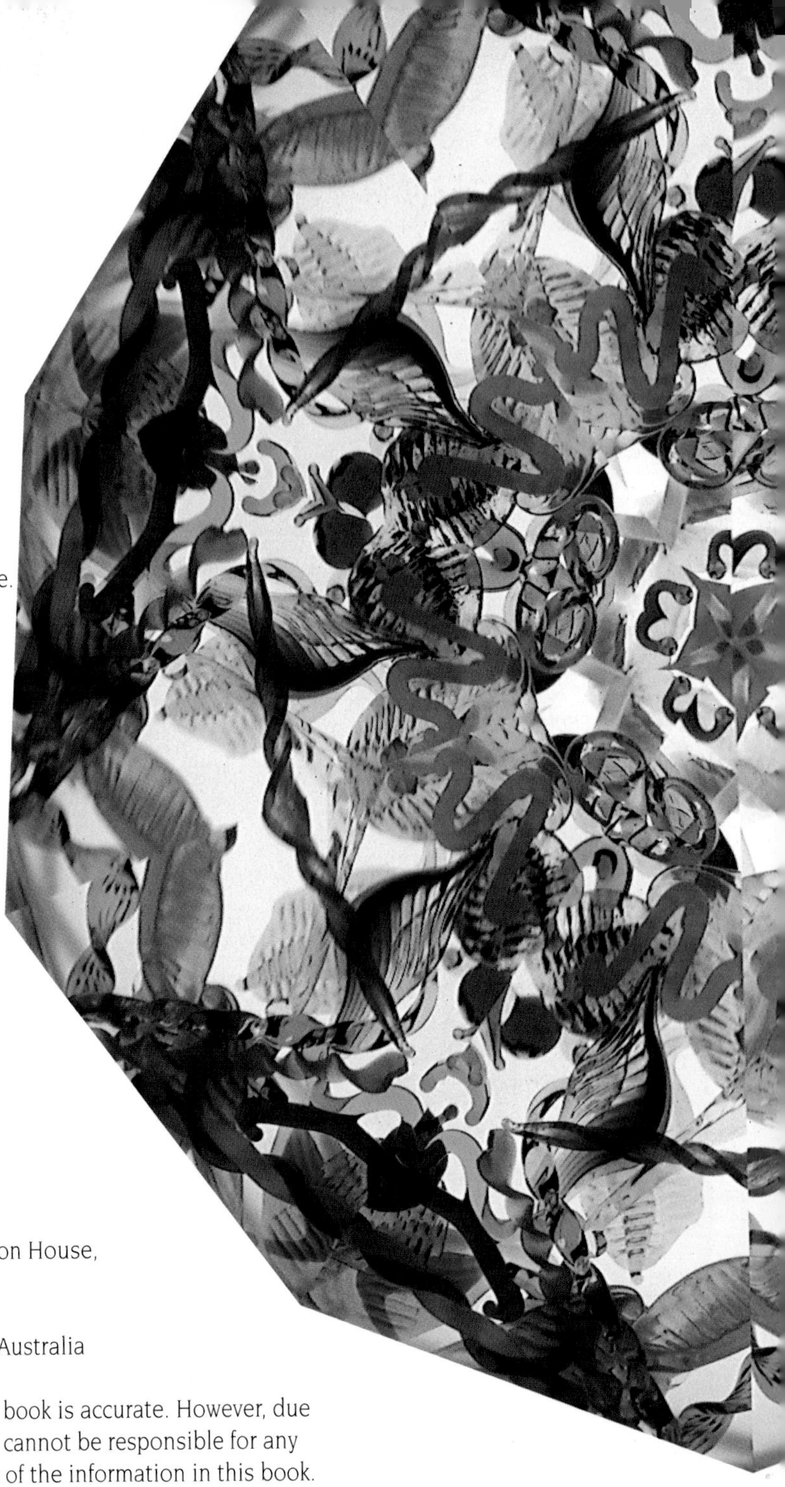

Editor: H.T. Boswell
Art Director: Kay Holmes Stafford
Photography: Evan Bracken, Richard Babb
Photographic Props & Assistance: Steve Brewer
Illustrations: Marc Tickle
Production: Kay Holmes Stafford

Library of Congress Cataloging-in-Publication Data
Newlin, Gary
     Simple kaleidoscopes : 24 spectacular scopes to make / by
Gary Newlin.
          p.   cm.
     "A Sterling/Lark book."
     Includes index.
     ISBN 0-8069-3154-X
     1. Kaleidoscope--Design and construction--Juvenile literature.
     I. Title.
     QC373.K3N49   1995
     688.7'2--dc20   95-4591
                                              CIP

10 9 8 7 6 5 4 3 2 1

A Sterling/Lark Book

Published in 1995 by Sterling Publishing Company, Inc.
     387 Park Avenue South, New York, NY 10016

Produced by Altamont Press, Inc.
     50 College Street, Asheville, NC 28801

© 1995 by Gary Newlin

Distributed in Canada by Sterling Publishing Co., Inc.
c/o Canadian Manda Group, One Atlantic Avenue,
     Suite 105, Toronto, Ontario, Canada M6K 3E7
Distributed in Great Britain and Europe by Cassell PLC, Wellington House,
     125 Strand, London, England WC2R 0BB
Distributed in Australia by Capricorn Link (Australia) Pty Ltd.,
     P.O. Box 6651, Baulkham Hills, Business Centre, NSW 2153, Australia

Printed in Hong Kong

Sterling ISBN 0-8069-3154-X

Contents

Preface

Cozy Baker

During the past decade there has been a keen resurgence of interest in kaleidoscopes. Allowing the eye to marvel, the mind to explore and the soul to soar, these mirrored tubes of magic have emerged as an important art form.

Since its invention by Sir David Brewster in 1816, the kaleidoscope has fulfilled a variety of functions. Universal in appeal and spanning all age groups, it has served as a toy for children, a center of parlor entertainment for adults and as a design palette for artists, jewelers, architects and weavers.

The current renaissance embraces an eager enthusiasm for learning the techniques involved in making quality kaleidoscopes that are creative and innovative.

For some, the kaleidoscope is a "happening"—a joyous experience—a celebration of color. For others, it is recognized and accepted as a valuable therapeutic and meditative device. Beyond its inherent beauty and captivating magic, the kaleidoscope symbolizes life...a succession of random interlinkings unified into one whole with new beauty being generated from the destruction of the preceding form.

Tom Chouteau looks inside his "Mirror Cube"

Life unfolds from the center.
New beginnings emerge from the
breakup of past forms.
All things turn and spin and change,
Endlessly rearranging themselves.
The world is truly a kaleidoscope.

Cozy Baker

A dazzling array of classic scopes from
the Cozy Baker collection.

Introduction

Have you ever wondered what makes a kaleidoscope work? How did they get this beautiful large image inside this small tube? Have you torn apart a toy kaleidoscope and found some pieces of plastic and shiny surfaces and wondered, "Is this all there is?" or "How did they do that?" Well, I have, and from this simple beginning starts a journey of incredible beauty and magic which can be taken to very advanced levels of sophistication or can be enjoyed in very simple ways. It is our intent in writing this book not only to give you ideas about what to make and how we made them, but more importantly to give you the knowledge to be able to figure out your own projects and do them with your own unique style. In our experimentation, both purposeful and just plain blind luck, we have discovered a great many ideas that run the gamut from wonderful and exotic to mediocre and awful. We will try to steer you in the right direction and are sure that you will find many of your own serendipities.

When one thinks about writing about simple kaleidoscopes the first thought is to go back to where you first encountered a mirror system and its magic, as it happened to you. Whether it happened when you first looked into a tri-fold dressing mirror in a clothing store, or you happened to look into two pieces of mirror that happened to be facing each other, you never forgot the image. Maybe you had a faint understanding of what was happening or maybe you had no idea at all, but the impact was unmistakable and unforgettable. This is what kaleidoscopes are all about. After many years of working with optics and mirrors there are still profound moments of discovery and wonder. Whether or not you know how it works doesn't matter, we all meet at the same place, we become a part of the kaleidoscopic image. For just as a kaleidoscope needs light, it must have a viewer for the magic to occur, and that makes us a part of the image. It is with this view that we write this book for you.

Whenever one pursues an idea, precision and the technical stuff are things that come after the initial burst of enthusiasm and energy. All that technical stuff is in the book. I encourage you to get right to the mirror system even before it is in its kaleidoscope body and experiment by looking at your world in a different way. It will never fail to amaze you as the most common items take on a totally different look when viewed through the mirror system. At this point it will occur to you that if everything you look at has a totally different appearance, you've got a lot of stuff waiting to be viewed in a different way. Even unsightly things come to have their own unique look when you look at things in a new way. Think about that idea for a minute, nothing has changed, just our way of viewing things. It is my wish that with this sense of adventure, hope, and excitement, you will enjoy this journey into the kaleidoscopic way of seeing things.

Two major ingredients in a kaleidoscope are the mirror system and the goodies that you put in the end chamber. Mirror systems are the "heart" of a kaleidoscope while the goodies may be regarded as its "soul". We will take you from the beginning, a reflective surface, on through tubular mirror systems, 1 mirror systems, 2 mirror systems, 3 mirror systems, 4 mirror systems and then on to unique tapered mirror systems and their fascinating cousins. Charles Karadimos, a nationally known kaleidoscope maker and a wonderful mirror system technician has written an article on mirror systems for this book, which you should read carefully.

After the rapture with mirror systems, we began to discover that the goodies you put in the object chamber can have a profound effect in the image you see. Years of experimentation and trial and error have lead us to believe that images are greatly affected by the dimensions of color, size, shape, texture, lack of color, transparency, opacity, filtering of light, scattering of light rays, blocking of light rays, and probably many other undiscovered ways of manipulating and reflecting light. Sherry Moser, another renowned kaleidoscope artist and inventor of the Chandala, The Journey and the Sphaera (all incredible and innovative kaleidoscopes), has written an article on the subject of what to put in the end chamber to create excellent images. This also deserves your attention.

One of the challenges of sharing the kaleidoscopic view with you is photographing the visual images. The human eye and brain see things differently than a camera lens. Our goal was to reproduce on film exactly what you would see with the eye. Much effort went into building mirror systems like the ones described in the projects, only much larger, to accommodate the camera lens. Mirrors in kaleidoscopes are of various types, the best being front surface mirror. We used front surface mirror for the photography in order to show you the best possible images as well as providing beautiful pictures for you to study.

The projects we chose to present to you represent a wide range of different types and styles from very simple to a few that are fairly complex. The first requirement for a project was that the materials be accessible to everyone. Often, for kaleidoscope bodies, we used common household items or containers one can easily find in local stores or businesses. The directions and dimensions for each project are written for certain sized containers. If you choose a different sized container, we show you how to measure and design mirror systems and object chambers to fit the size of container that you have. All kaleidoscopes work on the same principle no matter what the outside housing looks like. If you build a great mirror system and put excellent goodies in front of it, you've got an incredible kaleidoscope no matter how crudely it may be housed.

In making kaleidoscopes, it's the going as much as the getting there that's the fun and interesting part. In the process of building a kaleidoscope you will bump into some really fun things. Once you assemble the mirror system, it can be used as a teleidoscope to look at things around you. After assembling the kaleidoscope, figuring out what to put in the end chamber can be a great scavenger hunt. Math and science can be learned painlessly in this process.

Finally, you will find that a very large part of enjoying kaleidoscopes is in sharing them with other people. Try building a kaleidoscope with the whole family. With each exclamation "Oh, look at this one" from the sense of wonder at the endless succession of kaleidoscopic images, you will find kaleidoscopes to be very magical and wonderful instruments for bringing people together.

Simple Kaleidoscopes

All kaleidoscopes have certain things in common. The most important part of a kaleidoscope is the mirror system or otherwise reflective system that organizes the light rays into images. All kaleidoscopes have something to view, whether it is colorful objects in an end chamber or just viewing the world through a mirror system. Generally, kaleidoscopes have a body or housing to hold all the components together in an easily handled form.

Kaleidoscopes (scopes) may assume thousands of different shapes and looks but they all work on the same principle. After reading this book, whether you look at an expensive kaleidoscope and see an incredible image or an inexpensive toy scope, you'll have a very good idea of what kind of mirror system it has, and also what may be in the object chamber. This may break the magic spell for a moment, but the challenge and the inspiration will propel you forward to create wonderful scopes of your own design. You'll have the knowledge to design and construct all kinds of great scopes.

Let us guide you through these projects. Once you get the basic understanding of how to build a kaleidoscope, the ideas and energy will begin to flow in all directions.

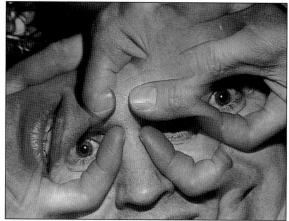

Photo: Joe Polevoi

Mirror Systems: The Heart of a Kaleidoscope

Any reflective surface can be used in a kaleidoscope to organize light. In a practical sense we use the term "mirror" for any of these reflective surfaces. When these individual strips are assembled together we call that a "mirror system". We'll use that phrase "mirror system" from here on.

Mirror Materials

Mirrors can take the following forms:

Paper and plastic mirrors
Polished aluminum, brass, or other shiny metals
Common 1/8" household type mirror
Clear 1/8" glass, plain or painted black on one side
Metal or plastic tubes
Front surface mirror

Paper and plastic mirrors

We have found a good inexpensive way to make mirrors that are safe and unbreakable. These mirrors are composed of stiff paper board and clear plastic. For the stiff paper you can use poster board, matt board (used in picture framing) or thin cardboard. The idea is to give the mirror a good flat backing which makes a better reflected image. Also, the thicker the sheet of plastic, the better the image because the thicker plastic reduces distortion. The best color for the backing board is white or pale blue, but other colors will work. These boards are then covered with a smooth clear plastic sheet which creates a reflective surface. Plastic sheeting can be found in different thicknesses and sizes. Our favorite plastic sheet is butyrate. Found in craft and hobby shops, it comes in 8" x10" sheets in a variety of thicknesses. The thickness that generally works best for mirrors is .015 mil. It has enough body to reduce distor-

tion and is cuttable with common tools. Drafting film is another option (make sure it has a shiny side, not a matt finish) and comes in large sheets, usually in a thin gauge. This is commonly found in drafting and blue-print stores. You may find other materials that will work for this purpose. The only requirements are that they be smooth on the surface for better reflections and that they are cuttable.

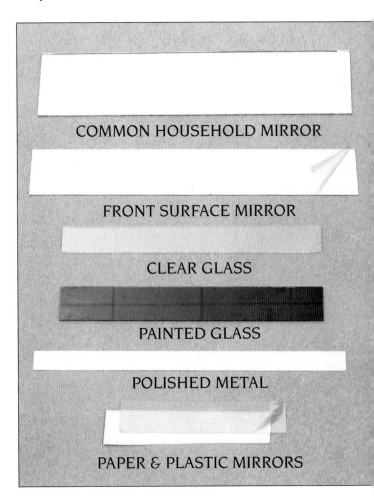

COMMON HOUSEHOLD MIRROR

FRONT SURFACE MIRROR

CLEAR GLASS

PAINTED GLASS

POLISHED METAL

PAPER & PLASTIC MIRRORS

To make paper and plastic mirror, cut your board to the size of the sheet you want to make, and spray a light coating of spray adhesive on the board. Press the clear sheet on top and press down. This mirror material can be cut with common cutting tools such as shears, a utility knife with straight-edge, or paper cutting board. If you don't have spray adhesive cut your board and your clear sheet to the size specified, and separately glue them together using tiny dots of glue in the corners. Press flat until the glue dries. Glue sticks also work well for this type of mirror.

Polished Metals

There are metals that come in sheets and strips. Aluminum and brass should be easy to locate. Often found in craft and hobby stores, these metals are thin enough to be cuttable or can be found in precut strips. The main requirement is that the surface be shiny and give you a clear reflection. Be careful of the sharp edges and burrs that may be on the edges of any metals.

Common Household Mirror

This mirror will work for a variety of projects and can be found everywhere. The best thickness of mirror is 1/8", called "double strength", or 1/16", called "single strength". If you are not versed in cutting glass, you can take your dimensions to a glass company or a stained glass store to have them cut it to size for you. Take precautions with any glass product to prevent breakage and injury by cuts.

Clear and Painted Glass

If you don't have mirror, regular 1/8" window glass can be used for mirror systems. Glass has a nice smooth surface for good reflections, and when enclosed in a scope's darkened body, it works quite well. You can paint the back of the glass with black paint if you wish. This will keep stray light out of the mirror system.

Metal or Plastic Tubes

Brass tubes found in hobby and craft stores often have a shiny interior and make great tubular mirror systems. Most plastic tubes have a naturally smooth inside and also work well for mirror systems. You may want to cover the outside of the tube to prevent light from entering through the body. Ideally you want light to come only through the end of the tube and reflect down the barrel to the eye.

Front Surface Mirror

Front surface mirror is the best mirror for kaleidoscopes. The reflective surface is on the front of the glass surface instead of behind the surface, as in regular mirror. This type of mirror gives the truest reflections and the prettiest images. The disadvantages of front surface mirror are the cost and the reflective coating, which is quite thin and fragile. Often, this mirror will be sold with a protective plastic coating on the reflective side. The most popular front surface mirrors have an aluminized coating which is deposited on the mirror under heavy vacuum. If the base glass is thin, it may be tricky to cut. For that special scope, you just might want to pay the price for front surface mirror.

Kaleidoscope Mirror Systems

Charles Karadimos

The magic of kaleidoscopes is based on the principle of reflection. Basically, what one is doing when viewing a kaleidoscope, is looking down the barrel of a mirrored tube. Therefore, it is the use of mirrors, the reflective principles of these mirrors, and their configuration that we must understand.

The idea of reflection is a relatively easy concept in terms of kaleidoscopes. Light travels in a straight line, strikes a reflective surface and bounces off that surface at the same angle at which it struck, continuing in a straight line until it strikes another surface, and so on. In a kaleidoscope, the procedure is basically to view some objects in the object case through a mirrored tube, with the mirrors producing a multiple series of reflections of the actual objects. This is very similar to the effect one gets when sitting between two mirrors, where the reflections bounce back and forth forever.

Many contemporary kaleidoscope makers use a special type of mirror to achieve the utmost image clarity. This mirror is called first surface or front surface mirror. First surface refers to the actual placement of a reflective coating on the top layer of the glass, providing a pure, unobstructed reflection of the light. A standard mirror, as we are all aware of, consists of a sheet of glass with a mirrored coating on the backside. As light strikes this type of mirror it must first strike the glass. The glass causes the light to refract or bend before it strikes the mirrored surface and then refract again as it exits the glass. This interference affects the quality of the reflection and the amount of the light actually reflected. Also, there is a slight reflection off of the glass surface itself. The resulting quality of the

image is therefore somewhat blurred. Since the actual image seen at the end of a kaleidoscope is the result of numerous reflections of one original pattern, the quality of the mirror is critical. This effect is eliminated with the use of first surface mirror. However, other problems do arise with the use of this material. Since there may be no protective surface on the coating, extreme care must be taken when handling. The cleaning of fingerprints and dust off first surface mirror can very easily remove the reflective coating. It is also very important that the mirrors have straight, clean cuts and are held together well to avoid a mirror seam where they come together. All of these things are much more important with first surface mirror than with plain mirror.

The mirror systems in kaleidoscopes can come in many variations. However, understanding the geometry involved in two basic arrangements, two-mirror and three-mirror, can help to build a foundation for other systems. Both of these designs have one thing in common; they are both set up in a triangular configuration, similar to a three-sided tube.

The two-mirror system is probably the easiest to understand. In a two-mirror kaleidoscope, the image produced is a central pattern surrounded by a black field. To achieve this, two mirrors are arranged as the two legs of an isosceles triangle in a "V" shape, with the third side of the three-sided tube being a non-reflective, usually black surface. By changing the angle of the "V", one can control the number of reflections and thus control the actual intricacy of the image to be symmetrical. Here is the rule of thumb for establishing the proper angle. Since the pattern in a two-mirror kaleidoscope is circular, start with the 360⁰ in a circle, divide that by the number of reflections you would like, say 8, for instance. The resulting angle is 45⁰. Thus, setting the angle at 45⁰ will produce 8 reflections or a 4-point star (two reflections creates one point). *See Figure* 1. Remember that any angle that divides the 360⁰ evenly, not fractionally, will produce symmetrical results. Here is a small list of other possible situations:

45⁰ *8 fold symmetry*
36⁰ *10 fold symmetry*
30⁰ *12 fold symmetry*
22.5⁰ *16 fold symmetry*
15⁰ *24 fold symmetry*
10⁰ *36 fold symmetry*
2⁰ *180 fold symmetry*

It is important that this angle be precise, otherwise the final outcome will contain only a part of the origi-

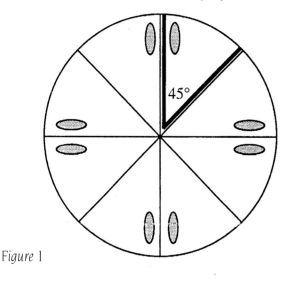

Figure 1

nal design at the last reflection and the image will not be symmetrically closed. Your eye is very discriminating and will pick up this flaw easily.

The three-mirror system creates an image that repeats one triangular pattern throughout the entire field of view. This system is indicative of many of the toy kaleidoscopes that have been available. The mirrors are arranged similarly to the two-mirror design, replacing the blackened side with a mirror. Pure symmetrical images are more difficult to achieve in this type of a kaleidoscope since there are 3 sets of angles that must now be accurate; not like the two-mirror system where only one angle is critical. Keeping the formula from the two-mirror system in mind, and also the fact that all three of the angles in a triangle add up to 180⁰, there are only three possible combinations of angles that will work effectively. The simplest is an equilateral triangle. The next is an isosceles right triangle, with angles set at 45⁰ - 45⁰ - 90⁰. *See Figure* 2. Here, two sides of the triangle are the same, with the third larger. The resulting image from this design resembles a repeated square pattern, with the square actually being produced by two triangles. The third and most difficult is the 30⁰ - 60⁰ - 90⁰ right triangle. Since all three angles and all three sides of this configuration are different, the alignment here is very critical. The resulting image however, is the most interesting and intricate. It produces a combination of 3-point, 4-point, and 6-point patterns, joined together in a honeycomb effect.

The descriptions above discuss the basic two and three-mirror systems, the goal of both, to produce pure, symmetrical images. However, very interesting

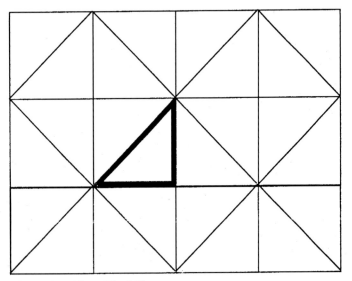

Figure 2: $45^0 - 45^0 - 90^0$

your eye. These are just a few of the other possibilities and combinations that can be created.

The above descriptions should help you understand some of the ways the more common types of patterns are created. It is the relationships of the two-mirror and three-mirror systems that determine the foundation for the overall workings of the kaleidoscope. After all is said and done, the kaleidoscope is a wonderful toy for creating colorful images. Understanding the science behind them should not detract at all from the *magic*.

results occur when the angles aren't quite exact, particularly in the three-mirror design. Geometric patterns are still produced, but the continuity is disturbed because the odd angles only show fractional parts of the image.

It is important to note that these aren't the only ways to manipulate mirrors in a kaleidoscope. Another variation may include 4 mirrors set up as a rectangular tube. The image that results here is a repeated rectangle, with the reflections moving up and down, and left and right. Tapering three mirrors from large to small and viewing from the large end, produces an image resembling a 3-dimensional sphere. Tapering a two-mirror system from small to large enables the system to allow more light to enter, and thus, effectively brighten the image, as well as enlarge it. A tube lined with mylar, a flexible, reflecting material, creates a spiraling effect that seems to climb up the tube right to

Assembling Mirror Systems

Before you begin to assemble a mirror system, get a clean non-scratching work surface. Wood is always a good surface to work on. If your work surface is hard, use newspaper to cushion the mirrors. Keep it clean to minimize dust, keep a dust brush handy, and keep other things from dirtying your clean mirrors. Before you position any mirror for assembly, make sure that they are as clean as possible. Finger prints, dust, or other things will show up in your mirror system, so keep the mirrors as clean as humanly possible and avoid touching the cleaned surfaces.

There needs to be a space between the mirrors to allow them to be folded into their formation. That space is equal to the thickness of the mirror that you are using. Use a piece of mirror as a spacer between the mirrors to set the gap.

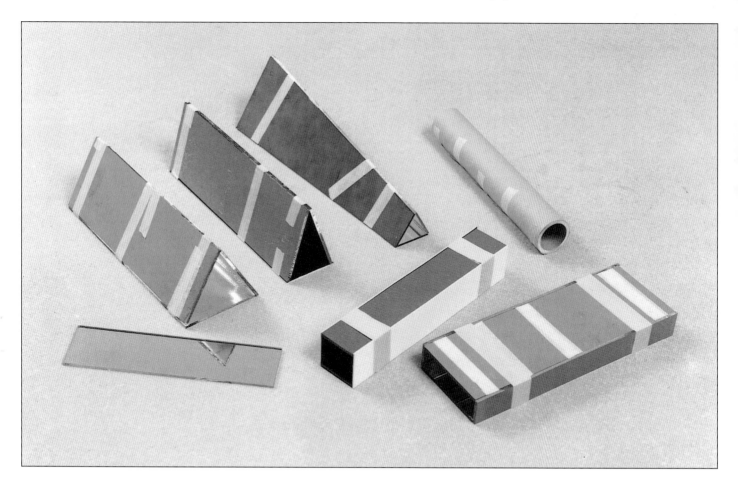

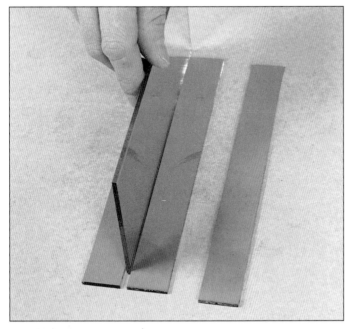

Step 1

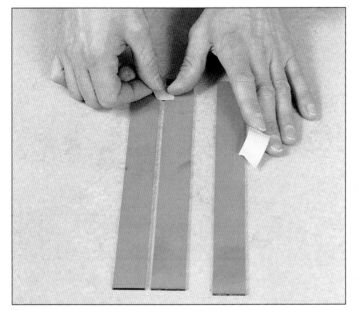

Step 2

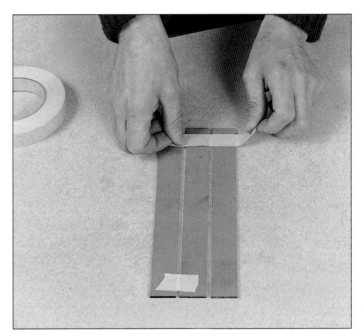

Step 3

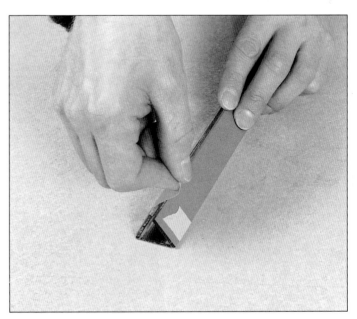

Step 4

Triangular 3-Mirror System

This mirror system is the most basic and easy to assemble. Lay your 3 mirror strips shiny side down, and line them up length wise. With a piece of the mirror, set the space between the strips and place pieces of masking tape as shown. Carefully turn the mirrors over and fold up and into a triangular shape as shown. Tape into place. You may want to hold the system firmly and put a strap of tape around both ends to secure the system from shifting. Once this is done you can start looking at things through the mirror system. The name for a mirror system that don't have objects in front of the system is Teleidoscope, through which you view things around you instead of looking at bits of color in the object chamber.

1-Mirror System

It is as simple as it sounds. It actually becomes a system when used in one of the upcoming projects.

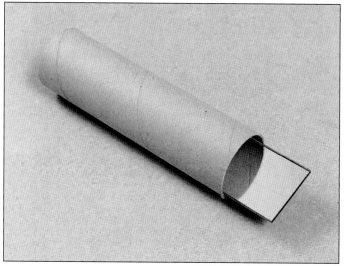

1-Mirror System

Spiral mirror system

Simply by looking down the inside of a shiny tube creates the spiraling effect. Some fascinating things can be viewed with this system. Most metal and plastic tubes have a smooth, clean interior.

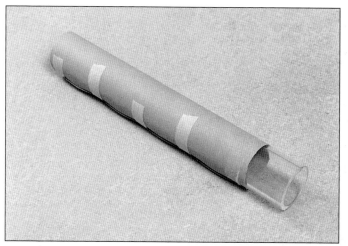

Spiral-Mirror System

2-Mirror System

Stick Trick

If you want to get perfect symmetry in your images, look through one end of the system and put a straight piece of wire or other straight material at the other end across the viewing area and touching both sides of the end of the mirror system.

While looking at the wire, move the free end of the mirror to different places on the card. In addition to giving you various numbers of "pie slices" you will find places at which the image you see is symmetrical. This could be any number of positions. When you find one you like, place a dot of hot glue on each end of the system and in the middle, connecting the mirror to the black cardboard. Hot glue is good because it sets quick-

2-Mirror system

2-mirror systems are probably the most popular systems. They give a mandala or pie shaped image, and you can control the number of "pie slices" by the angle at which you set the mirrors. These systems have 2 strips of mirror and a black cardboard. Usually black matt board works well, though you can make your own black surfaces in other ways. To assemble this system, proceed as in the triangular system beginning with the 2 mirror strips next to each other and the black cardboard at one side. When you turn the strips over, let the black cardboard be on the bottom. You can change the angle of the 2 mirrors by placing the free mirror anywhere on the black card. *See diagram.*

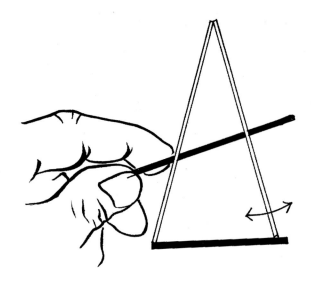

Stick Trick

ly. You may want to over-coat the hot glue with epoxy to further strengthen the bond, and add masking tape after the glue is set to further secure the system. 2 mirror systems require off-center eye holes. Size of the viewing area may become a factor. Experiment with different angles to find the one that suits you best.

Tapered Mirror System

This system creates an outstanding spherical image.

You've got to try it to believe it! A tapered mirror system must be drawn and cut precisely to prevent gaps in the mirror system. The assembly is much like the equilateral triangle format. Lay out the mirrors as shown and fold them up into an equilateral triangle shape. The tapered system has a very large view port or eye hole, and can be utilized in larger projects as well as small ones. If you have someone else cut your mirrors, take them a precisely drawn template to use as a pattern.

Tapered Mirror System

Square Mirror System

This creates an interesting point of view. Everything is in little square boxes, all over the place. Assemble this system just like the others. Fold up and form a square. Two of the mirror strips will sit on another mirror and the other two will sit off the edge of the mirror. *See diagram*. If you are careful you can tilt this mirror system to form diamonds instead of squares.

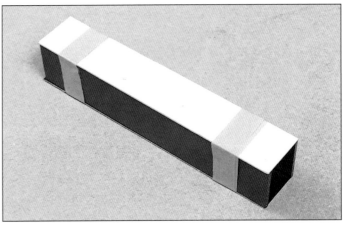

Chorus Line Mirror System

Chorus Line Mirror System

This system was developed by Corky Weeks and, with her permission, we have taken liberties with it in this book. Images in this system travel from one side to the other. The effect is created by using a square mirror system but substituting 2 black cardboards for 2 of the opposing mirrors. Lay the mirrors out: mirror, black cardboard, mirror, black cardboard, and assemble as in the square mirror system. If you add a slight taper to the black cardboards you will get an image that pushes toward you in the center and falls away as the images go into the distance.

Square Mirror System

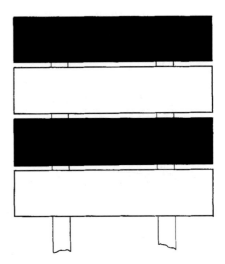

Sizing Mirrors

Sizing Mirrors for Different Sized Tubes

When you find a tube or body that you want to use, the first question that comes to mind is how wide should the strips of mirror be. To save you the effort of trial and error to find the size, we have some formulas that work with 1/8" mirror. If your mirror material is thicker or thinner you can make small adjustments in the formulas for the differences in thickness. A simpler way of guesstimating the width of the mirror strip is to cut a cardboard mock-up of the size you think it should be. Try it on for size and adjust as necessary. One of the considerations in determining the width of the mirror strips is that you usually don't want the mirror system to contact the side wall of the body because of possible breakage if the unit is dropped. The formula allows some room for padding or packing. Also, if the mirrors extend all the way to the edge of the body you may get some parts of the body in the viewing area which you don't want. These formulas will give you room to adjust and center the mirror system where you want it.

How long should your mirror strips be?

In many scopes the object chamber is inside the body of the kaleidoscope. In others, the object chamber or other viewing objects may be on the outside. In the case of a wheel scope or a scope that has an end cell, the mirrors will be the length of the entire body minus the thickness of the protective eye piece covering plus the thickness of the end cover. *See diagram.*

As with most things, minor errors can occur in measuring. It is wise to be a tad smaller than larger. With mirror systems, if they are a bit short you can usually make adjustments at the eye piece end with no difference in the viewed image.

If your scope has an internal object chamber, the mirrors will be shorter than the length of the body of the scope to allow room for the object chamber, as well as the circles on either end of the body which hold the goodies. In general, 1/2" to 3/8" subtracted from the length of the mirrors is adequate. These measurements give you enough room for the width of both circles, and allow enough space for the goodies to tumble and create their images. If you have very thin goodies (like feathers or flower petals), you need less space in the chamber, and likewise for larger goodies you need more room.

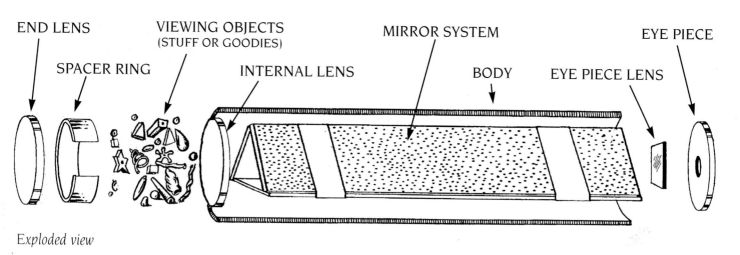

END LENS SPACER RING VIEWING OBJECTS (STUFF OR GOODIES) INTERNAL LENS MIRROR SYSTEM BODY EYE PIECE LENS EYE PIECE

Exploded view

Measuring & Taping

Formulas for 1/8"(double strength) mirror

Measure the inside diameter of the tube or body that you are going to use. Inside diameter (ID) is the measurement from one inside wall to the other inside wall. You are measuring the diameter of the inside opening of the tube. Take this measurement and plug it into the formulas below.

For equilateral triangle format (3 strips): .68 inch

For 2 mirror system (2 strips in a tall triangle shape): .75 inch

For 4 mirror system, square or chorus line: .60 inch

If your mirror material is 1/16" thick instead of 1/8", add .05 inch

Example: If your inside diameter is 1.25 (or 1 1/4) inches and you want to use a triangular mirror format, 1.25 times .68 = .85. Make it simple: .85 is real close to .875 which is 7/8". The width of the strip should be 7/8" wide. These formulas work for round scope bodies. If you have square or triangular bodies you can pretty much measure the openings and allow a little for the thickness of the mirror you are using and allow for the packing or padding to cushion the mirror system.

What is the best length for a mirror system?

The length of a mirror system is important to the image that you see. Mirror systems shorter than 5 to 6 inches may be hard for the eye to focus on and may require a magnifying lens. There is an ideal range or ratio of length of the mirrors to the size of the mirror strips. For instance, if the mirror strips are 1" wide (in an equilateral triangle format) and the length is 6" long, the image you see will be six pie slices and a little portion of the next ring of images. The original image will jump out at you and you probably can't enjoy the image as a whole. If the same mirror system is 15" long you will see a lot of small images, probably too small to really enjoy. Through experimentation, you will find certain ratios of the mirror's length to width that will produce nicely proportioned images that are neither too big or too small.

Taping Mirror Systems

Masking tape is a good tape to use, both in the initial taping to hold the strips in place on the table, and later when the system is folded into position. After folding the mirror system into position it is good to hold the system firmly together and apply a little more masking tape to ensure that the mirrors aren't loose and can't slip out of formation. You will want to secure both ends of the mirror system and the middle if it seems loose or moves around.

After taping the mirrors in position, look into the system. If you see light coming through the seams, tape down the seam lengthwise with black plastic tape to prevent light from leaking in. When taping mirror systems together, try to avoid overlapping the tape more than 4 or 5 times. If there is too much tape, the mirror system may not fit into the tube. In the taping and packing processes take care and see that no tape or other material intrudes into the viewing area. All you want to see in the viewing area is tumbling objects.

We have found that masking tape works well for taping mirror systems. It doesn't stretch like plastic tapes do, and inside the body of a kaleidoscope the tape is kept away from sunlight so the tape doesn't dry out. Black plastic tape, or electrical tape, is excellent for sealing out light.

Packing & Padding

Most mirror systems are fragile and should be protected from accidental breakage. There are several ways to pack a mirror system. Two of the best are: rolling the system up in 1/8" styrofoam sheet, and packing small pieces of styrofoam packing peanuts into the spaces between the mirror system and the side wall of the scope body. When packing by either method, the goal is to pack the system snugly so it doesn't shift and move about in the body. There is a balance between securing the mirror system and packing so tightly that the mirrors break or distort the view. A good way to test your packing is to gently shake the system, if the mirror system slides out, you need more packing. In addition to securing the system, packing also allows you to center both the eye piece end and the viewing end. When you use foam sheet, cut your sheet almost as long as the mirror system, that way you can center both ends. If you use pieces of packing peanuts, be sure to pack both ends and pack each space(between the mirror system and body wall) about 3-5 pieces deep.

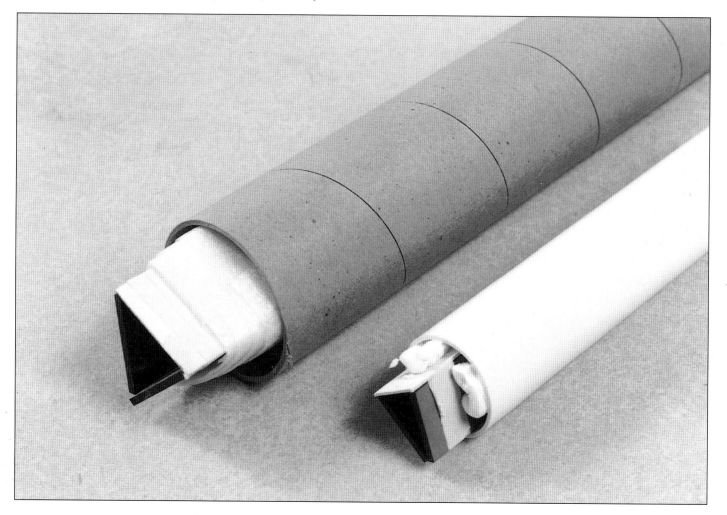

Lenses & Eye Pieces

All scopes have clear or translucent material at each end. At the eye piece end, the viewing end, the material is clear so one can look into the mirror system. Generally, there is a clear circle or other shape to hold objects in the chamber, and finally on the end there will be another circle or shape which may disrupt light rays or give a pattern to the viewed image. In the case of wheel or marble scopes, this may vary. *See diagram on page 21.*

Materials that may be used for eye pieces and other lenses are .030 butyrate plastic sheet or an unbreakable polycarbonate of a sturdy gauge. Polycabonate sheet can be found in stores that sell plastic rod, sheet, and tube.

Eye Piece End

The primary use of an eye piece lens is for **protection of the eye**. Glass mirror systems or other glass parts can break and become dangerous. A good sturdy plastic or unbreakable eye piece is essential. Do not use glass for the eye piece! We suggest always using an eye piece. In addition to providing protection, the eye piece helps keep dust out of the mirror system.

Here is a collection of things which are good end lens materials.

Internal Lenses

Most scopes that have an internal object chamber have a clear circle (or other shape) inside the body that may sit on the end of the mirror system. This circle keeps the objects contained in the object chamber, keeping them from falling into the body of the scope or in the mirror system. Generally, this circle is clear but can be frosted or textured for certain effects.

End Lens

This is the lens that you can have fun with. Often, you see scopes that have a frosted lens at the end. This type of lens is used to diffuse the light rays coming in to give a soft white, contrasting background for the colorful material to tumble inside the object chamber. Another reason to use a diffusing end lens is so that you don't see things in the environment which might distract you from the image.

If you are using clear sheet plastic, try scratching the surface with sandpaper to get a translucent look. You can also score designs into the plastic for certain effects. Stained Glass stores will have a great number of textured glasses that will work for end lenses. Don't forget that you can use colored glasses and plastics as end lenses. While you are at the Stained Glass store, ask to see some glass jewels and cabuchons (smooth dome type jewels). Both jewels and cabuchons do wonderful things when used as the end lens. These can also be used as the end lens in a teleidoscope.

Polarizing filters make amazing lenses. These filters let light through only on a certain plane. When you put polarized filters in the place of the end lens and the inside lens and add bits of clear styrene (CD cases, tape cassette boxes, tape dispensers, crumpled cellophane)

you get an explosion of color in violets, blues and ambers. Certain plastics, like the neck of a soft drink container, show really unique and excellent images when added to a polarized end chamber. *See photo on page* 112.

If you make small kaleidoscopes, you may need a magnifying lens. The human eye doesn't focus very well below 5-6 inches in length, and it helps greatly if you use a magnifying lens in the eye piece end of the scope. Magnifying lenses have different focal lengths, so you'll need to match the lens with the length of your scope. A common reading magnifier, made of sheet plastic, will work for certain lengths and is inexpensive. You can tell focal length by putting the sheet up to your eye and looking at something. When it comes into focus, that is your focal distance.

Triangular 3-Mirror System

1-Mirror

Square
Mirror

Chorus Line

3-Mirror
Tapered

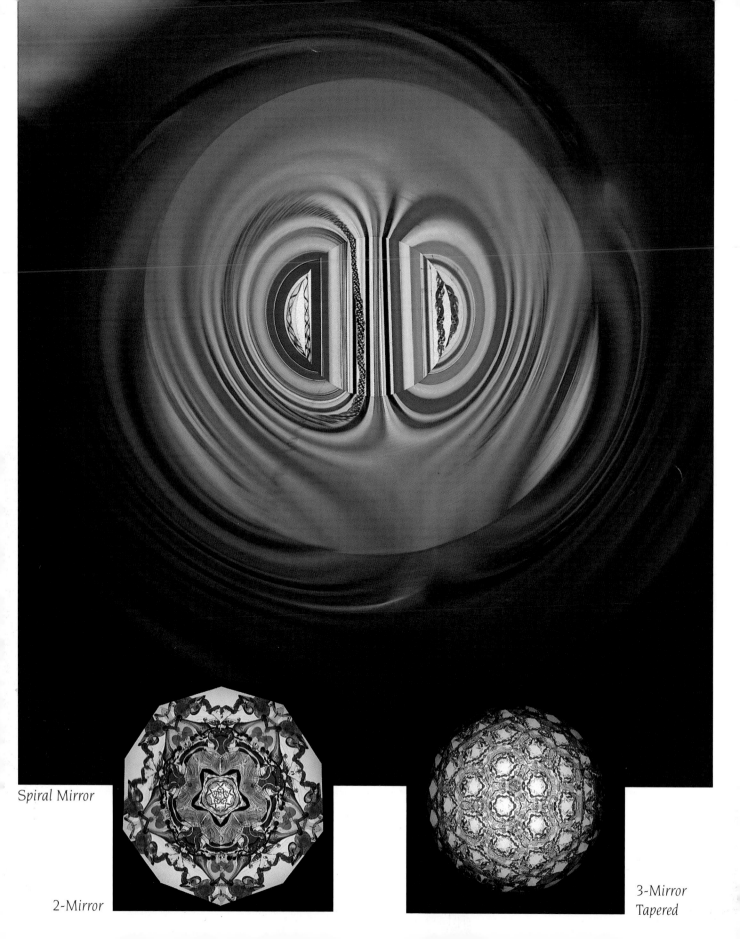

Spiral Mirror

2-Mirror

3-Mirror
Tapered

Barrels & Other Bodies

Body Size and Shape

Kaleidoscope bodies can take a multitude of forms and sizes. There are two general classes of scopes, hand held scopes you bring to your eye and larger scopes which sit on their own legs or base, where you bring your eye to the scope. When you start looking for material for your scope you begin the search for a container or tube that can be held easily in the hand, has enough room inside to contain the mirror system and packing, and is long enough for the eye to be able to focus. You may need more room on the inside of the body than you think.

Most often scope bodies are round, which makes them easy to handle. The round tube shape is a very strong and sturdy one and easily adapts itself to all kinds of scopes. A general rule of thumb for selecting body size is: 7 to 10 inches in length and 1 1/4 to 2 inches in diameter. Tubular bodies offer the greatest selection of materials. Cardboard tubes are readily found and often come with some type of end cap. Metal tubes can be found in shapes other than round, including square (tubular furniture legs) and triangular shapes. Rectangular boxes offer a fun variation in body shape. A rectangular shape, like a video cassette box, will need a different shape of mirror system and can be a fun challenge.

If your scope is housed in a large body it will need some form of support or legs to sit on. This type of scope is called a parlor scope. The name parlor scope comes from the 1800's, when most of the scopes were too large to be hand held and were attached to a base. These parlor scopes were often displayed and enjoyed on a table in the parlor or sitting room. When you design the legs or base for a parlor scope, make the angle of the body so that the viewer can sit at a table and comfortably look into the eye piece as well as reach the other end to move the object chamber or cell.

Body Materials and Decoration

Probably the most accessible and inexpensive scope body is the cardboard mailing tube. Mailing tubes can be found in all sizes and diameters and thicknesses, some with colorful outsides, and sometimes with two end caps which can be utilized as eye pieces and end caps. Mailing tubes are easily cut to size and can be decorated with different colors of construction paper, which can be glued to the tube with white glue. These tubes also work very well with fancy tapes, glitter and glue, wrapping paper, or comics from the Sunday newspaper.

The grocery store is a wonderland of kaleidoscope body material. Food is packaged in a variety of round and rectangular containers in both cardboard and plastic. You may even find that the printing on the package is an excellent outside decoration.

Plumbing supply stores offer tubes in various metals, often with matching end caps. Another material used in plumbing is PVC tubing, and it too can be fitted with end caps. Either of these tubes come in a wide range of sizes, from pocket model size to large parlor scope size. One of our favorites is 1 1/4" hard copper tubing (DWV, drainage, waste, and vent, if you can get it) with matching end caps. The copper can be polished with abrasive hand pads to remove the oxidation and dirt, and then polished with metal polish to get a great shine. Copper parts can also be dipped in a polyurethane coating to preserve the shine. Polyurethane is a clear coating that is used on hardwood floors, and provides a protective layer to keep the copper from staining. It also gives a pretty sheen to the scope body. Various chrome plated tubes can be found in the plumbing departments of home improvement stores. A chrome plated tube will not stain or discolor and is often light weight, making it an ideal body for a scope.

PVC tube is great material for a durable, light, and inexpensive scope. It is also a good material for creating a liquid-filled cell. Silicone sticks and seals to PVC readily. The printing that comes on the tube can be removed with steel wool and alcohol. Various types of end caps can be had for all sizes of PVC tube. Extra large PVC can make a giant size parlor scope or an interactive scope. PVC is also cuttable and workable for legs and stands on scopes.

End caps are handy and easily used in scopes.

However, finding caps that match the size of tube that you are using is sometimes a wild goose chase. You will find that you may find a cap in an auto parts store, and find the matching tube in a local hardware. Tubes are sometimes fitted with protective coverings which exactly match the tube. Usually, the protective caps are thrown away when the tube is used in its application. If you can get someone to save these for you, you have a kaleidoscopic gold mine. Chairs that are made of tubular metal usually have plastic caps on the ends of the legs. If you find one of these chairs, you can cut the legs off for bodies and use the plastic caps as eye pieces and end caps. If end caps are not easily found you can cap off the end of a tube with 1/8" plastic glued into place on the end of the tube. You might also tape the end plastic pieces in place with colorful tape, or use copper foil and solder to secure the end if you are familiar with stained glass soldering techniques.

The search for scope body material is a fun task that can be enjoyed by the whole family. You will find excellent body material in the most unusual places.

Stuff

Sherry Moser

The dictionary gives some of the definitions of stuff as (1) constituent elements of basic nature, essence (2) things grouped together or viewed in a certain way (3) to fill the inside of something (4) to pack, cram, or crowd something into a container. So it's appropriate to title this chapter as "Stuff." The object chamber contains the most important components of the kaleidoscope besides the mirror system. The stuff that is chosen for the object chamber determines the unique image that is created through the mirror system chosen for your kaleidoscope. Let's talk about stuff.

There are a number of factors that affect the image. The most important factor is your own imagination and creativity. There are endless possibilities. Do not necessarily be influenced by what has already been done by other artists. Often things will happen to create a great new image by playing around with objects or concepts that you do not have any idea what the look will be until you try it. Some great images have been created in just this way. Be open to all sorts of possibilities.

Let's consider some of the elements that influence the look of your image. The size of your pieces plays an important part. Very small pieces create a delicate and lacy look. Larger pieces give more color and a bolder look, and not as complex an image. Smaller pieces mean that it will take more pieces to fill the object chamber. Balance is the key. Use a combination of large and small pieces, such as tiny seed beads to large chunks of broken glass. Do not over-fill your cell because pieces will not have enough room to rotate freely. When the cell is too full, the image will not change as dramatically because the pieces cannot

tumble and allow other pieces to pass the mirror viewing area. On the other hand, not having enough pieces in the cell allows too much open space in the mirror so the image is not full. A general rule of thumb is to fill the cell at least half to two-thirds full. Temporarily seal the cell so it can be turned and rotated while looking at the image to determine if pieces need to be taken out or added.

Pieces, no matter what they are made of, should be translucent in nature. Light should be able to come through to some degree. Wonderful natural things that people find intriguing to put in object cells are shells, rocks, and minerals. The problem with these kinds of items is that a majority of them are opaque with no light coming through. An occasional shell or rock will work because enough light comes in around other pieces. Things that are opaque look dark, and too many dark items will darken the overall look. Just try to balance the cell with a little bit of many different kinds of things.

Colors have a very profound effect on all of us. Color plays a significant role in our everyday lives whether we realize it or not. Each individual has their own personal perception of colors and the value and meaning of these colors. There are many books available about color and color theory. However, to start, pick the colors that are personally pleasing, but do not be afraid to experiment. I have looked at many scopes where artists used color combinations that I personally would not have picked, but created the most wonderful images. Do use bright colors, and stay away from dark colors such as browns. A little ribbon of black, however, can be a striking contrast to rich jewel tone colors. I cannot say it enough, just experiment and experiment until the look is achieved that is pleasing to you, the creator of the piece.

There are no rules written in stone about what to use for pieces. All the pieces do not have to be the same kind. If glass is used, one does not have to use all glass pieces. Many artists who choose to use glass use only glass, but there is no reason that it has to be done this way. Some other things to consider for choices will be discussed in the following paragraphs.

Plastic beads are plentiful and can be found in most craft stores along with small glass seed beads. These kinds of beads are relatively inexpensive. Even more fun is to raid your grandmother's jewelry box for some vintage costume jewelry to use as exciting objects for your kaleidoscope. If a special scope is being made for someone, why not take personal items that can be included in the object cell. An example might be a charm from a bracelet, or initial beads form a newborn's identification bracelet. Visualize the idea, then find items that make the scope very personal.

One of the most obvious choices for the object chamber is glass. The question is: how do you want to use this glass? One can wrap small pieces in a towel or newspaper and crush them with a hammer to make small pieces of colored glass. If you have clear glass separating the mirror system and the object cell, there is the possibility that these broken or crushed bits of glass over time can scratch the clear glass. To go a step further, take your broken bits of glass and put them in a rock tumbler to round off the edges. A glass kiln for fusing glass will also round the edges of your glass, making the pieces nice and nugget shaped.

Lampworking is another technique for working with glass that allows glass to be heated over a flame. As the glass becomes soft and molten, it is twisted and shaped to add texture and shape to the glass. Many of the current contemporary kaleidoscope artists are using lampworking techniques to create their very special look. Each artist develops a style of working with the glass that becomes a sort of signature and is recognized by collectors who value their work.

Stained glass techniques of foiling glass pieces and soldering them together to create wheels that rotate on a spindle can be used instead of an object chamber. Usually, two wheels are applied and rotate independently of each other to show crossing colors and patterns. Pressed flowers or flower petals sealed between glass also offer beautiful colors and texture to the image. Flower petals have a tendency to fade over a period of time so should be protected if possible from sitting in bright sun light. These wheels may need to be replaced at some point. Wheels are a good place to use agates and semi-precious stones.

Every day items that add interest to object cells are simple things like paper clips, safety pins, springs, watch parts and filigrees. Again, remember that solid objects that do not let through any light will be dark and opaque. Use these kinds of items sparingly. More non-traditional items that can be considered are seeds, feathers, leaves, or even possibly insect wings or bodies. Please consider how fragile these items are, and as the object cell tumbles whether pieces falling against each other will cause some of these items to disintegrate over a period of time. Is the object cell going to open so that these items could be replaced if need be?

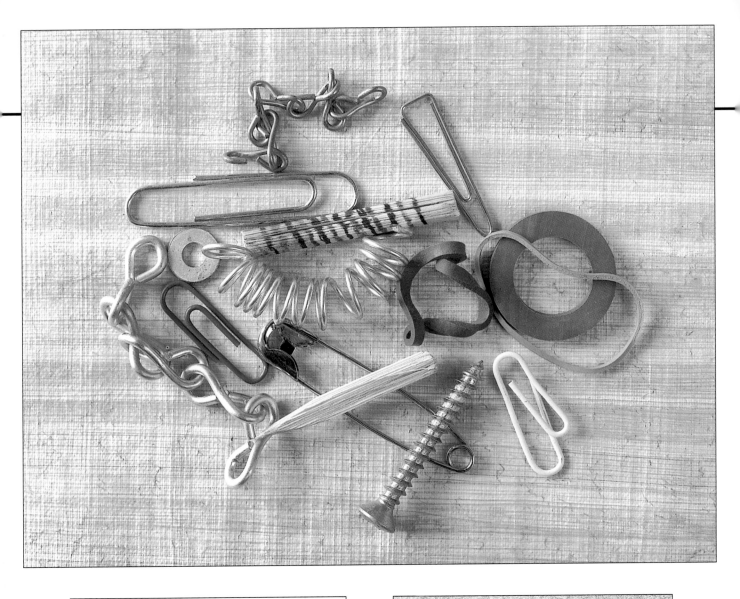

Colored papers which allow light to come through can be used. Paints applied to plastic films offer other alternatives. Plastic films imprinted with a logo are a great way to advertise. Pictures imprinted on the plastic films can help create a theme scope such as bugs, butterflies or just anything. I know there must be many other kinds of stuff that could be included in the object chamber. Be open to trying most anything, and be on the look out for that special something like a sparkling antique button that catches your eye all the way across the room. Mostly, be creative. Being creative can be very hard work but the rewards are worth the effort. We all have the ability to be creative, but we must develop it and help it grow.

I discussed a little bit about the "stuff", but lets talk now about other things that are a factor in creating the image. The light source is most important as it illuminates the chamber and the pieces for viewing. Natural sunlight is the best source to give the truest colors. However, sunlight is not always available, and some artists build into their kaleidoscopes hidden sources utilizing flashlights to pinpoint light into the object chamber. To enhance viewing of the chamber, a frosted white background focuses the view only on the pieces in the chamber. A clear background would allow the viewer to see beyond the object cell pieces to see outside the chamber into the surrounding room. Many people do not like a clear background as it muddies the image. Teleidoscopes are kaleidoscopes without a chamber, and the view is exactly what you see when you look around a room but reflected through the mirror system.

Kaleidoscopes which offer side-lit chambers can add to the amount of light in the chamber. Black background chambers must have side light to illuminate the cell since no light comes through the black side. Artists using these cell concepts add sparkling pieces that give the image an almost fireworks kind of look.

Chambers can be a part of the body of the scope with a small area at the end reserved for the object cell. The depth of this area is important and is related to the width of the kaleidoscope body. You do not want to see the sides of the object chamber in the mirrors. If that happens, your cell is too deep for the width of the chamber. Also, if the chamber is too deep, more pieces will be needed to fill the chamber. Chambers can be totally separate for the kaleidoscope body and attached at the end.

Up to now, the discussion has been about adding pieces to what is called a dry cell. In a dry cell, the pieces tumble freely against each other and create a very unique sound as they tumble. Another option for object chambers is to create a liquid cell. Pieces float in a heavy liquid that gives an ongoing movement to the image, even when the cell is not being rotated. Most often-used oils are mineral oil and glycerin, which are available at any drug store. The trick in making a liquid cell is that it must be totally and completely sealed to prevent leaking. Not an easy task. As beginning scope makers, I would recommend sticking with the dry cell concept for now, or wheels. Dry cells allow the artist to make a cell that can be opened to allow the interchange of pieces, therefore creating a new kaleidoscope image every time that pieces are interchanged.

One final definition from the dictionary on stuff is (5) to fill with information, ideas, etc. [to stuff one's head with facts]. Hope this little chapter is not too much stuff to deal with, but will help to jumpstart you with lots of ideas.

Goodies for the Object Chamber

There are a lot of things you can use to create beautiful images in scopes. One of the colors often overlooked is clear. Clear objects can do two important things. One: clear objects separate the colored goodies and add clear spaces in the image, resulting in a lighter, lacier image, and two: clear elevates the colorful goodies into the viewing area of the scope. In the exciting hunt for colorful transparent goodies, you might find that you overlook color schemes of all one color. Some of the most beautiful images are made with different shades of the same color mixed with clear to elevate and separate.

The following list will get you started in your search for goodies:

Colored stained glass from specialty stores	Screws
Crushed glass	Springs
Broken glass	Paper clips
Cut glass	Chain links
Flame-worked glass for clarity and round edges	Washers
Hand made beads	Rubber bands
Marbles	String or yarn
Jewels and rhinestones	Screen wire
Round glass balls or beads	Copper wire bent to shape
	Filigrees
	Watch gears and parts
Plastic beads-from specialty stores	
Round and faceted beads	Flower petals and stems
Oval beads	Leaves
Tri-beads	Twigs and thorns
Star or spoke shaped beads	Insect wings and bodies
Wooden beads	Feathers
	Seeds
Plastic films	Seashells
Colored paper	Wood shavings
Pipe cleaners	Agates
Plastic or paper colored with markers	Semi-precious stones
Sunday newspaper comics	
Translucent paint on clear plastic	

Object Chambers, Cells & Wheels

The definition of an object chamber is a space in the kaleidoscope that contains the viewing material or objects. In this space the objects must be able to tumble freely as the chamber is rotated or moved. A great number of scopes have these internal object chambers.

Cell, Object Chamber, and Wheel

One of the questions that will occur to you is how deep the object chamber should be. Light must be able to come through the objects and on through to the mirror system. If a chamber is too deep, several objects may pile up together and not allow much light in. The result is a dark or black image. A general rule of thumb is for the depth of an object chamber to be 1/4" to 3/8". The size of the objects may determine how deep the chamber should be. If you are using thin objects like feathers or paper, probably 1/4" will do, while shells or other, thicker objects will need 3/8". Remember that the objects should tumble while the chamber is rotated. If there is not free motion the image will hang up and not change frequently. Motion is affected by size and shape.

Object Chambers

Object chambers generally use a spacer or spacer ring to keep the inside circle from falling into the objects or pushing them against the end lens. The spacer ring can be made from a section of the tube you are

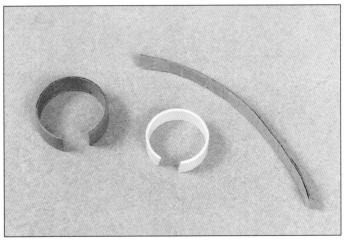

Spacer Rings

using for the body. You'll need to cut a portion of the spacer ring away so you can squeeze it together and slide it into the object chamber. You can also cut strips of thin cardboard and form them into a circle and insert into the chamber. Spacer rings or strips need to be thin enough so that they don't intrude into the viewing area of the mirror system. If you look straight into the object chamber, you can see the viewing area. Anything that is in front of the mirror system will show up, and anything beyond the system will not be seen.

Some of our projects have objects inside the mirror system. This is a wonderful version of goodies. They roll to you and away from you, and can be part of the image or not. Goodies in the mirror system allow you to look at the same objects in many different ways.

Cells

Cells are enclosed cases which contain tumbling goodies and are attached to the body in various ways.

Cells are very similar to internal object chambers, the difference being that they are separate from the body of the scope, and usually turn independently of the body.

Cells are constructed like internal object chambers, keeping your viewing area clear of spacer rings. Depth of the chamber itself will be like the internal chamber. A quick way to make a cell is to cut off a portion of the tube you are using and glue two clear circles to either side of the slice of tube, creating a cell.

Wheels

Wheels are free spinning circles which are attached to the body of the scope. These wheels have the goodies glued or attached or sandwiched between two circles. Wheels are turned in front of the mirror system to produce images. When you construct a wheel it must cover the entire viewing area so you won't see the edge of the wheel in the viewing area. Often, wheels extend beyond the body of the scope, and you may need feet to keep the wheels from bumping when the scope is set down. Wheel scopes can have more than one wheel. You might have a color wheel and a clear texture wheel, allowing you to change the color and the texture at the same time. Wheels are traditionally thought of as vertically spinning wheels, but a horizontal spinning carrousel or a horizontal cell is also a possibility.

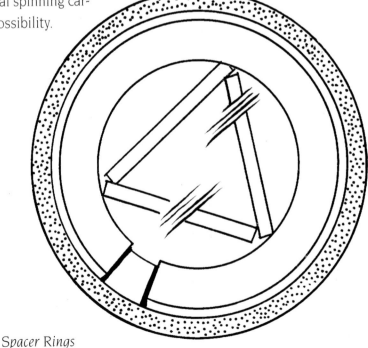

Spacer Rings

Adhesives

Over the years of building kaleidoscopes and mirror systems, we have found certain adhesives that tend to do the best job of kaleidoscope making. Whether it be tape or glue for holding mirror systems, glues for securing circles in place, or otherwise getting something to stick somewhere, we offer the following suggestions along with our reasons for using them.

Tapes

Our favorite, masking tape, is an excellent tape for taping mirror systems together. Masking tape has a tiny bit of "give" when you need it, but doesn't stretch like electrical or black plastic tape does. Masking tape can be untaped easily for adjustments, a definite plus. Several laps of masking tape survive well in the darkened body of a kaleidoscope. Very little ultra-violet light gets into the body of a kaleidoscope. Masking tape will stay flexible and hold for a number of years. Black plastic tape is excellent for sealing light out of mirror systems. Colored plastic tapes, available in bright colors, can be pretty decoration as well as doing a tape's job.

Glues

Clear silicone is one of the best glues. It is cantankerous, ornery, and otherwise aggravating to deal with, but has great qualities of flexibility and the ability to stick to almost anything. Silicone has a unique ability to stick to slick surfaces like plastics, which have been difficult to secure with other glues. Scopes get handled quite a bit, and the flexible nature of silicone is a definite advantage. It can be cut away if you need to remove it.

Here's how to deal with silicone. Buy a small tube of silicone (not a canister that requires a mechanical "gun" to apply) with a replaceable screw cap. The replaceable cap will save you from buying and rebuying silicone because it cured in the tube. Go to the feed and seed store and get several 12 CC syringes. If you need pinpoint accuracy, buy a couple of 14 or 16 gauge veterinary needles and cut the sharp point off. When you want to use the silicone, load 3 or 4 CC of silicone into the syringe at a time. When you come back to use the silicone in the syringe and you find it to be cured, throw the syringe away- that's right- throw it away and and get a new syringe. Believe me, waste and energy considered, it's cheaper to throw it out. The only disadvantages of silicone are the curing time and that it tends to pull out a little stringer of silicone when you pull back from your work. Practice will take care of the little stringers. If you get silicone where you don't want it, don't wipe it, let it set and cut it away. Read precautions about contact lenses and silicone, which are on the side of the tube.

Low temperature hot glue has come to have a valuable place in the delicate operation of setting the angle in 2 mirror systems. You can put a small dot of hot glue to secure the mirrors in position. It sets very quickly and will hold the position until you can reinforce the system with tape. Another advantage of hot glue is that you can remove it easily if you need to. The ability to put small amounts of hot glue in delicate situations, along with its fast setting time, make it a great glue.

5 Minute Epoxy

A good old standard glue, it is easy to handle and sets up rather quickly. Its qualities of setting hard and solid are an advantage in some cases.

For general gluing situations, you can use good old white glue and contact cement. They work fine for a lot of situations such as gluing paper to cardboard tubes.

Cat Scopes by James Dana Hill

Fruit & Veggie Scopes
by Chuck Nelson

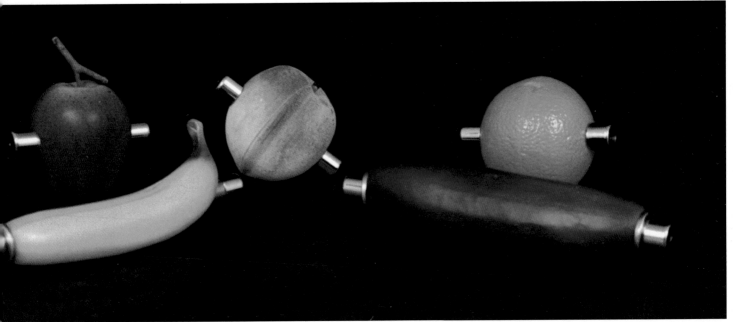

Bejeweled Egg Scope by Barbara Mitchell

Cosmic Eggs Scope
by Barbara Mitchell

Kaleidoscope Wagon
by Tom Chouteau

Pie in the Sky
scope by Tom Chouteau

Hall of Mirrors
by Tom Chouteau

Tall Corn State Building
kaleido-periscope
by Tom Chouteau

Interior of the *Kaleido Aquarium*

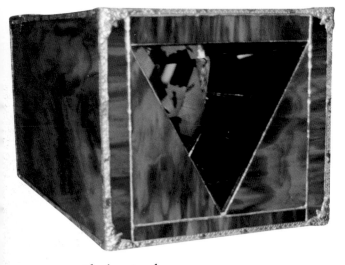

Kaleido Aquarium
by Tom & Sherry Rupert

Up Through the Roof
kaleidoscope by Bruce Haney

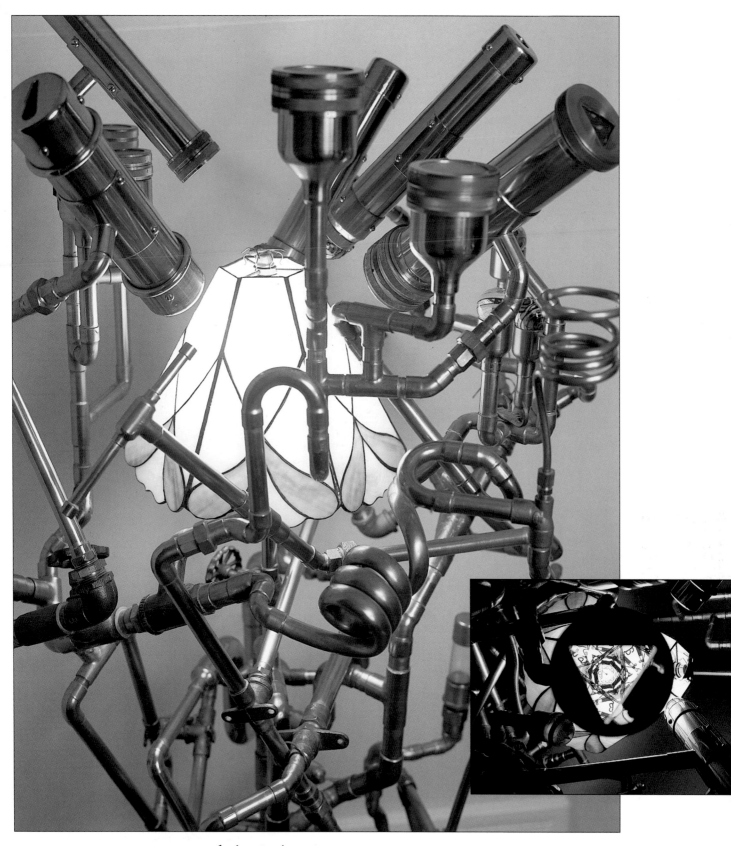

Kaleido Lamp by Dan Sudnick

Sphere
with 9-point image by
Charles Karadimos

Party time(s) Six on a rotating base by Charles Karadimos

48

Interior of *Dichro Delta*
by Charles Karadimos

Tessera
with 4 simultaneous images
by Charles Karadimos

Squash Lovers
viewed through
the Bennett scope

Footbridge in Golden Gate Park,
San Francisco

Footbridge viewed
through Bennett scope

Photo: Joe Polevoi

Photo: Joe Polevoi

Photo: Joe Polevoi

Photo: Joe Polevoi

Children's Hospital, Akron Ohio,
with 3 views
through a Bennett scope

Garnet Firefly
by Greg Hanks

Kaleido Plane
assortment by Greg Hanks

Poly-angular Kaleidoscope
by Wiley Jobe

Interchangeable components

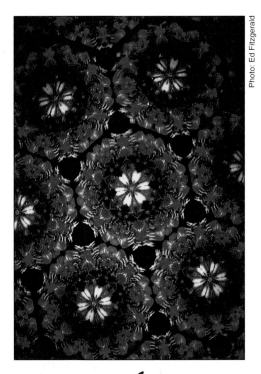

Photo: Ed Fitzgerald

Interior view of *Spirit* scope
by Luc & Sallie Durette

Fanta Sea
by Luc & Sallie Durette

Interior of
Talking Animals

Talking Animals 2-system musical scope by Debbie Brodel & David Rosenfeldt

Playground blocks panel
in Cleveland Park

Blocks panel
through Bennett scope

'57 Chevy tail light through
Kaleidovision camerascope

Pumpkin roadstand

Pumpkins
through Bennett scope

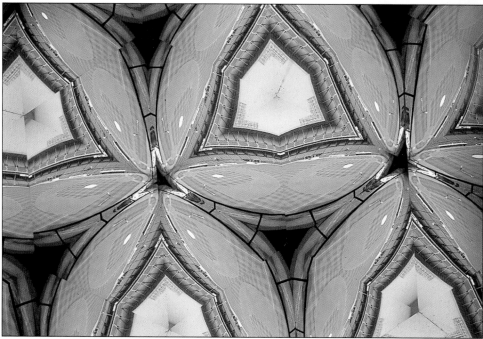

Baseball stadium
through Bennett scope

Parlour scopes & other kaleidoscopes
by Marc Tickle

Geiko Scope
by Marc Tickle

Photo: John Flowerdew

The Pinnacle
by Marc Tickle

Interior of
Parlour Explosion
by Marc Tickle

M-60

by Skeeter & Pete DeMattia

Victorian Sun
by Skeeter & Pete DeMattia

Brass & Chrome
by Skeeter & Pete DeMattia

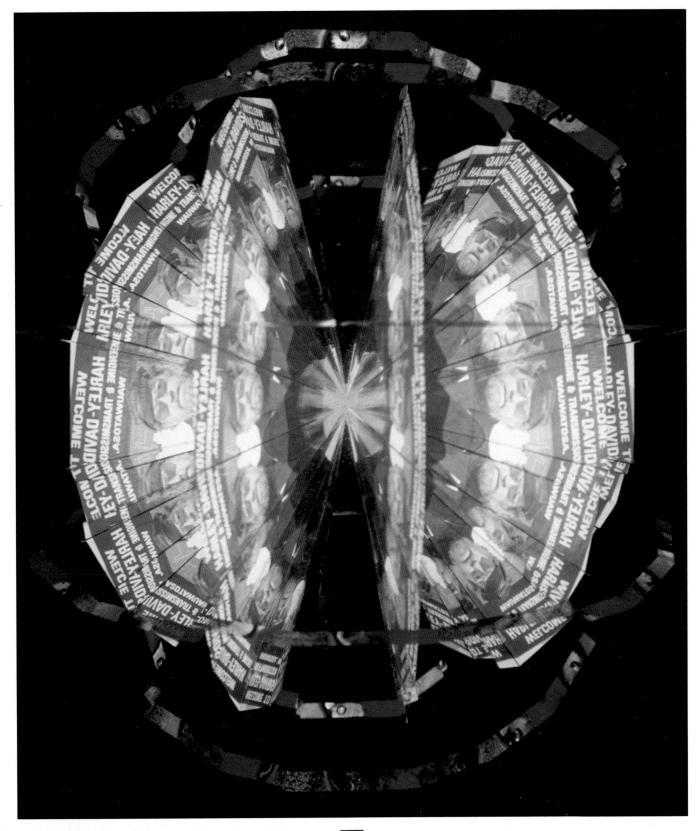

Kaleidosphere 2 by Don Doak

Kaleidosphere 1
by Don Doak

The Incredible Willmeister by Willie Stevenson

Silk Dancer a musical poly-angular scope by Willie Stevenson

You are cordially invited to join The Brewster Society, an association for collectors, designers, and sellers of kaleidoscopes.

A quarterly newsletter keeps you up-to-date on who's who and what's what in the world of kaleidoscopes and where to attend exhibitions, shows, and regional Brewster meetings.

An Annual Convention is held for meeting artists and fellow enthusiasts, sharing ideas, learning, and previewing newly created kaleidoscopes. There is also a wholesale buyer's show for retailers.

The Brewster Society
Studio B - 9020 McDonald Drive
Bethesda, MD 20817
(301) 365 - 1855

Cozy Baker, founder of the Brewster Society

The Projects

Tumbling Spiral

Tumbling Spiral

Here's the kitchen version of the spiral mirror system. We've added goodies which roll back and forth inside the mirror system. Through practical experience, kids also find these scopes to be great noisemakers when shaken, and also become drumsticks at times.

Materials:

1 Paper towel roll, trimmed to 10" long
1 Sheet of drafting film, or .0075 clear butyrate,
   5" x 10"
Clear plastic wrap (microwave type wrap is sturdier)

Assembly:

1. Assemble the round mirror system by rolling up the clear drafting film or butyrate, and slide it into the paper towel roll.

2. Cover one end of the tube with a double layer of clear plastic wrap, about 4" x 4", and tape the wrap down with masking tape so it doesn't come off the end of the tube.

3. Put about 5 to 10 plastic beads into the open end of the tube. Cover the end with clear wrap and look at the images. Add or remove beads until you get the mixture you like.

4. Secure plastic wrap over the other end as in step 2, and you're ready to decorate the tube.

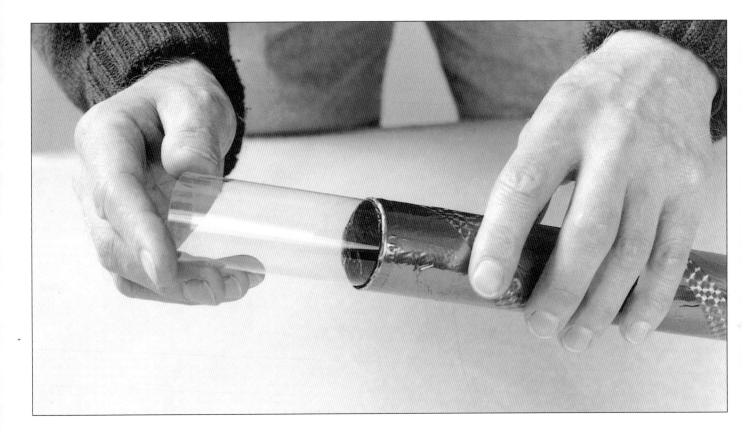

Fuzzy Worms

With a slight change, this same paper towel roll becomes a wheel scope.

Materials:

1 Pencil with eraser

2 Rubber bands

5 Large multi-colored pipe cleaners

Assembly:

1. Construct the paper towel roll as in previous project, leaving off the plastic wrap.

2. Take 4 pipe cleaners, hold them together, and wrap half of the other pipe cleaner around the middle of the bundle to hold them tightly. Wrap the other half of the pipe cleaner and wrap it tightly around the eraser end of the pencil.

3. Bend the pipe cleaners at angles or curl them around. Use the 2 rubber bands to secure the pencil to the outside body of the scope.

Wiggle or turn the pipe cleaner bundle in front of the circular mirror system.

Simple Teleidoscope

This type of kaleidoscope, which doesn't have an object chamber, is called a teleidoscope. It takes everything you look at and breaks it up into kaleidoscopic pieces. By pointing it at everyday things, you get a very different view of the world. You must try eyeball-to-eyeball: two people look into opposite ends of the scope at the same time. Also try looking at the "ear scope", "hair scope", "tooth scope", "shoe scope", "jewelry scope"... you get the picture.

Materials:

1 Paper towel roll trimmed to 10" long

3 mirrors 10" long x 7/8" wide

Clear plastic wrap (microwave type wrap is sturdier)

2 18" lengths of shoe string, ribbon, or cord

Assembly:

1. Assemble the mirrors in a triangular format.

2. On one end of the paper towel roll, punch 2 holes on each side of the tube. Insert the string or cord and knot it so it won't pull back through the hole. Do this for both holes.

3. Insert the mirror system into the tube and cover each end with clear plastic wrap. Tape the film down so it won't slide off the tube. You're ready to decorate the towel roll.

Fuzzy Worms

Simple Teleidoscope

Scope Neckline

Scope Neckline

This scope goes with you wherever you go, around your neck. A wearable kaleidoscope is a fashion statement.

Materials:

1 Toilet tissue roll
3 mirrors 4" long x 5/8" wide
1 cardboard spacer strip
    1/2" wide x 3" long
1 piece .030 clear butyrate plastic sheet
36" length of cord for the necklace

Assembly:

1. Cut the toilet tissue roll lengthwise, flatten it out and cut to 3" x 4 1/2"(the length of the roll). Roll back up into approximately a 1" tube and tape together.

2. Trace around the outside of the tube and cut 2 circles of .030 butyrate for each end.

3. Using the other clear circle as a model, cut a clear circle that will fit down into the tube.

4. Trace around the eyepiece lens onto a piece of cardboard, cut it out, then cut a hole in the center. Glue the lens to this.

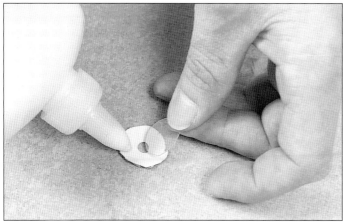

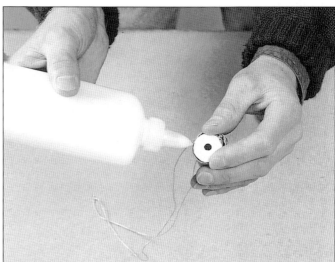

5. Assemble the mirrors into a triangular shape. Pack the mirror system, and slide it into the tube.

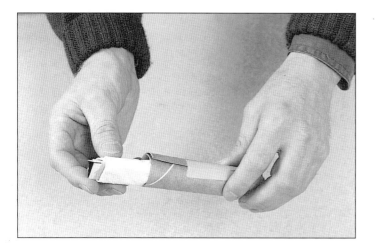

6. Stand the tube on its end and slide the mirror system all the way down.

Place the smaller clear circle on top of the mirror system, and form the cardboard spacer strip into a circle. Tape together and slide into the tube.

7. At this point, load some goodies into the object chamber, tape the end circle (lens) on and see if you need a magnifying lens in the eye piece end. If not, use the clear plastic circle. After doing this you can glue the eye piece end and the end lens in place with silicone.

8. Before you decorate the tube, take 3" of each end of the necklace cord and glue to each side of the tube. Glue them all the way down.

Hint:

Because of weight, use paper and plastic mirrors.

Twirling Club Sandwich

Whirling Doilies

Twirling Club Sandwich

Save those toilet paper rolls and fancy toothpicks. Nothing goes to waste.

Materials:

1 Toilet paper roll

2 mirrors 3/4" wide x 4 3/8" long

1 Black cardboard 1/2" wide x 4 3/8" long

2 Clear plastic circles of .030 butyrate, (one lens cut from a reading magnifier if needed)

17 Frilly toothpicks

2 Rubber bands

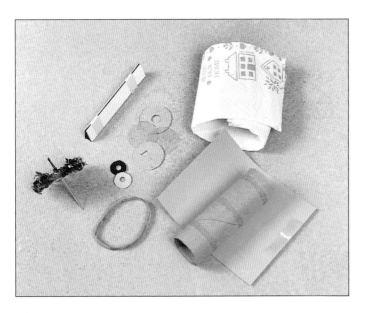

Assembly:

1. Assemble the mirrors and black cardboard into a 2 mirror system.

2. Trace the outline of the end of the toilet paper roll and cut 2 clear circles.

3. Pad the mirror system and secure it in the tube. Glue the clear circles on each end.

4. Cut off 16 frilly toothpicks 1/4" below the frill, leaving 1 toothpick uncut.

5. Cut 2 circles of thin cardboard the size of a dime, and punch a small hole in the center of each with a toothpick point.

6. Lay one of the cardboard circles down and run a bead of white glue around the circle, taking care to keep the punched hole free of glue. Arrange the cut ends of the toothpicks so the ends are in the glue and the frills stick out and form a wheel.

7. After the glue has set, put another bead of glue on the other circle and place it face down on the cut ends of the glued toothpicks. Line up the punched holes and slide the uncut toothpick through to line them up. Let the glue dry.

8. When you decorate the body of the scope, cut paper circles the same size as the clear end circles and cut out the triangle for the eye piece end and the other end.

9. Use the 2 rubber bands to hold the uncut toothpick to the side of the roll.

Variants:

Use toothpicks with no frills and glue or hang objects from the wheel.

Whirling Doilies

Interchangeable wheels give you many kaleidoscopes with only 1 body and mirror system.

Materials:

 1 Salt box with the pour spout removed
 2 mirrors 5 1/4" long x 3" wide
 1 Black cardboard 5 1/4" long x 1 1/4" wide
 1 Clear plastic circle 4 1/4" in diameter with a hole in the center slightly larger than 1/8"
 1 Bolt 3/4" long and 1/8" in diameter
 2 nuts to fit the bolt
 2 washers 1/2" in diameter to fit the bolt

Assembly:

 1. Cut the top of the salt box off, remove the pour spout, and save.

 2. In the other end of the salt box, cut a hole 1/2" in diameter in the center of the bottom of the box.

 3. Assemble the mirrors and black cardboard into a 2 mirror system.

 4. Take the cut off box top and place the mirror system on the box top. Center the mirror system, and trace an opening for the mirror system and cut it out. Make sure to cut away the pour spout hole.

 5. At the mark, punch a small hole for the bolt to go through. Take the bolt, add the washer, and push through the hole from the inside. Add another washer and a nut, and tighten down.

 6. Pack the mirror system and place it in the box. Put the top lid in position, lining up the mirror system with the triangular cut out, and tape in place with masking tape.

 7. Take the clear plastic circle and paint or decorate. Slide the wheel on the bolt and put the last nut on to hold it in place. Take it for a test spin.

Variants:

Try these variations on wheels:

Paper doily wheel, colored with markers or crayons
Plastic disk, acrylic paint — you will be amazed what translucent paints will do!
Plastic disk with glued on fabric swatches
Crocheted doily with fabric stiffener
Plastic disk with glued on stuff
2 Plastic circles encased wheel: feathers, paper, insect wings (encased wheels will protect fragile things) secured with silicone around the edge
2 Wheels, 1 with textured clear contact papers, and the outer wheel with colored goodies

Batteries Not Included

Multi-system Observatory

Any old box will do. Stick in a bundle of mirror systems, put feet on the box and you've got an interactive scope. Objects can be "played with" in front of the mirror system. In this type of scope you can bring in larger

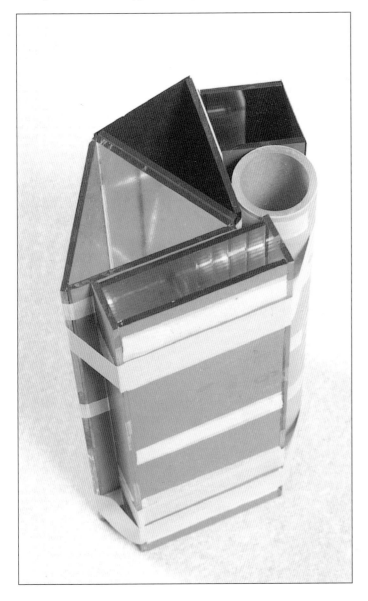

For this project we grabbed a 9x12x12 cardboard box, measured how deep the box was, subtracted about 1/8" for the clear plastic view ports on each end and made all the mirror systems that length before bundling them together. When the mirror systems are bundled together you can guesstimate what size opening to cut in the bottom and the top of the box. Cut a clear plastic sheet, 1/8" thick to fit the entire bottom of the box, and drop it in. Put the mirror systems in place and tape the systems to the sheet of plastic, all the way around. Fill the rest of the box with packing chips, add another sheet of 1/8" clear plastic the size of the entire top of the box, fold the flaps in over the plastic sheet and tape the box lids down. Add feet, in this case plastic containers. They need to be tall enough so that you can get your hands into the viewing area. There's no telling what you might find to put into the viewing area of this scope.

objects and opaque objects as well. You may want to cast a little light in from the side to light up opaque things.

Batteries Not Included

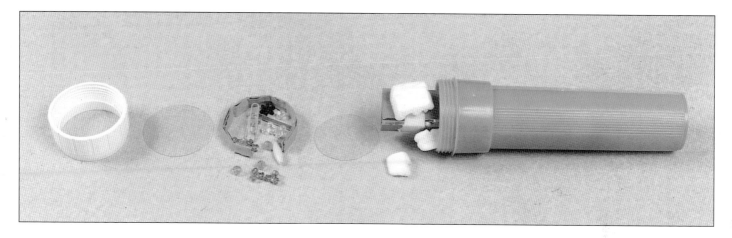

Cleverly disguised as a flashlight, this scope can be enjoyed in lots of places where work should be done. Most come with a pre-cut disk exactly the right size for this project.

Materials:

Plastic flashlight(2 D cell type) 7 1/4" long and. about 2" in diameter on the largest end

1 1"x1" square .030 clear butyrate

1 circle .030 clear butyrate, 1 3/4" in diameter

1 disk which comes with the flashlight, already cut to size

3 strips mirror 1"x 6 1/8"

1 cardboard spacer strip 3/8"x 5 1/4" long

Assembly:

1. Open flashlight and remove the reflector and bulb assembly, save the bulb as a spare.

2. For the eyepiece, drill a hole 3/8" in the center of the bottom of the flashlight body.

3. With a screwdriver, reach down into the bottom of the flashlight and bend the brass contact back against the wall of the flashlight.

4. Drop the 1x1 clear square into the flashlight and shake it about until it sits flat over the eye hole.

5. Assemble mirrors into an equilateral triangle format and slide into the tube.

6. Pack mirror system so it doesn't move in the flashlight.

7. Take the 1 3/4" clear disk and sit on top of the mirrors.

8. Form the spacer cardboard into a circle and place in the flashlight on top of the clear circle.

9. Add goodies.

10. Place the disk that comes with the flashlight on the end, and screw on the end of the flashlight.

Variants:

This scope will adapt to a 2 mirror system. You will need to off-set the eye hole, avoiding the bent brass contact, and substitute a round clear disk in the place of the 1x1 square.

If your flashlight is a different size, use the .68 figure times the inside diameter of the flashlight body to get the width of the mirror strips. Adjust your circle and square, and measure the depth of the flashlight, leaving 1/2" for the end chamber and the disks.

Double Vision

Double Vision

This two-in-one scope is a treat for the eye, as well as a study in mirror systems, embracing the best of both worlds.

Materials:

1 Potato chip can with plastic lid
1 Extra lid
3 Strips of mirror 1 3/4" x 8 7/8"
2 Strips of mirror 2" x 8 7/8"
1 Black card 3/4" x 8 7/8"
2 Clear circles of .030 butyrate, 2 3/4" in diameter
1 Cardboard spacer strip 3/8" x 8 1/2" long

Assembly:

1. Assemble the 3 mirrors 1 3/4" x 8 7/8" into an equilateral format.

2. Assemble the 2 mirrors 2 " x 8 7/8" and the black card to form a 2 mirror system.

Be especially careful to avoid oily fingerprints on your mirror system, since you may be eating the chips while assembling the mirror system.

3. With a can opener, cut away the metal end on the potato chip can. It might be advisable to wipe out the inside of the can to remove any oil that may remain on the sides of the can.

4. Slide the two mirror systems into the can. Line the systems up and apply a spot of glue or tape to secure the mirror systems to each other at both ends.

5. Take one of the clear disks and put it in the eye piece end, then put the cap on and stand the can on the eye piece end.

6. From the other end, push the mirror system down all the way into the can.

At this point you may want to pad the mirror system or glue it in place.

7. Place the other clear circle down in the can and add the spacer ring.

8. Back on the eye piece end, hold the scope up to the light and mark where to cut the eye holes in the lid. Remove lid and cut the openings.

9. Remove the clear disk from the eye piece end and glue the mirror systems to the wall of the can. When dry, replace clear disk and lid.

You're ready to load the goodies.

Hint:

This scope has a large object chamber. It is a great experimental chamber. You can also play with the depth of the object chamber. We put two mirror systems in this one, but if you plan carefully you can get three or more mirror systems inside.

Free Wheeling

A fast and fun scope, with enough wheels to take you anywhere you care to go.

Materials:

2 mirrors 8" x 2 1/4"
1 Black cardboard 8" x 1 3/8"
1 Clear plastic circle .030 butyrate 4 3/4" in diameter
2 Triangles clear .030 butyrate cut to size
1 Piece of stiff wire like a coat hanger
2 Marbles or the like, for feet

Assembly:

1. Assemble mirrors and black cardboard into a tall triangle.

2. Bend the last 1/4" of the wire into an L shape.

3. With the mirror system sitting on the black cardboard, glue the wire along the top of the triangle so that the end of the L sticks up and extends a bit past the end of the mirror system. The wheel should slide onto the end of the L and hang straight up and down.

4. Trace the openings on either end of the mirror system and cut the .030 butyrate to size, then glue onto each end, sealing the mirror system.

5. Cut the 4 3/4" clear circle and drill a hole in the center just slightly larger than the diameter of the wire. It is important that the wheel extend just beyond the viewing area of the mirror system to prevent the edge of the wheel from being seen.

6. Glue the 2 marbles onto the bottom of the wheel end of the scope. This will elevate the scope body so the wheel doesn't hit the surface it sits on.

7. Glue stuff onto the clear circle and take it for a test spin. The stuff should be on the front of the circle so the back of the circle can fit snugly against the scope body and turn freely.

Variants:

This scope is a great one to sandwich feathers, leaves, dried flowers, or any other fragile things into the wheel. Cut 2 circles, load your goodies, and glue together with several dots of silicone on the edge of the 2 wheels.

Create 1 wheel with only clear textures, clear contact paper in textures, or etch/scratch designs into the plastic with sandpaper or an etching point.

Quadruple Taper with Dancing Balls

This neat little scope creates quite an illusion with rolling and dancing clear balls inside the mirror system. Its larger cousin is based on exactly the same principle, but has an added feature of a horizontal rolling end chamber.

Materials:

2 mirrors 5" long, tapering equally from 2" down to 1"

2 mirrors 5" long, tapering equally from 1" down to 1/2"

2 Rectangles of .030 butyrate cut to fit each end of mirror system

5 to 7 tiny, clear glass or plastic round balls or beads (approximately 2 to 4 millimeters)

Assembly:

1. Assemble all 4 mirrors together, wide ends together and small ends together. Fold up into a rectangular shape and tape together.

2. Measure or trace openings on each end of the mirror system, and cut butyrate or plastic sheet into rectangles of the proper size to cover the openings. Glue one plastic rectangle end in place.

3. Add clear balls into the mirror system and glue the other clear rectangle into place.

Wow! When you get through studying the little dancing balls, you'll notice that this scope is a wonderful teleidoscope with a spherical image. After that, you'll notice that each end of this scope has a uniquely different view. Double Wow!!

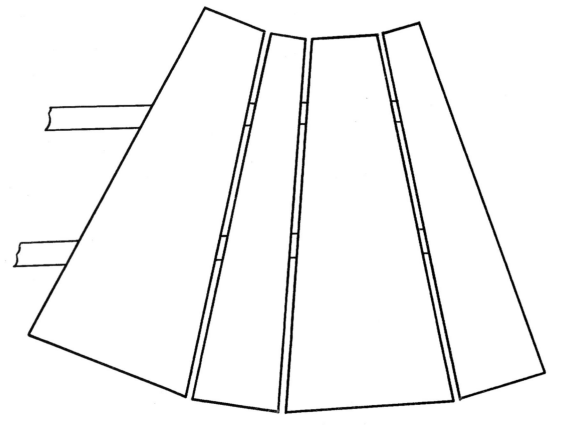

Big Quad Taper with Cylinder

We've added some features to this model. It becomes a kaleidoscope because we have added goodies in the horizontal rolling cell. On the outside covering we used matt board and added cut outs for the forehead and nose so you can get your whole face into the visual area and block out light from the side. This creates total kaleidoscopic immersion.

If you would like to make this one, just double the measurements for the mirrors, tape 2 rectangles onto the end of the scope to hold the rolling cell, and form the cut outs for the eyes and nose. Triple Wow!!!

Quadruple Taper

Tapered Kaleid-oat-scope

Tapered Kaleid-oat-scope

After you've added some fiber to your diet, cook up this feast for the eyes.

Materials:

    1 Box of oatmeal, preferably with a plastic lid

    3 Strips mirror 6 1/2" long, tapering from 3 1/8" at the large end to 1 1/4" at the narrow end

    2 Clear plastic circles of .030 butyrate, cut to the size of the inside diameter of the oat box

    1 Translucent plastic circle of .030 butyrate to fit the outside diameter of the oat box, or use the plastic lid if you have it

    1 Spacer strip of cardboard, 3/8" wide 10 1/2" long

Assembly:

1. Assemble the mirror strips into a tapering mirror system.

2. Open the oatmeal box, save the oatmeal. Place the large end of the tapered mirror against the unopened end of the oatmeal box, center it up, and lightly trace the outline of the mirror system.

3. Cut out this triangle 1/8" on the inside of the traced line. You don't want to see the edges of the mirror when you look into the eye piece end.

4. Drop one of the clear circles into the box. Place the mirror system (large end) into the box, and line the system up with the triangular shaped opening.

5. Apply some silicone at the 3 points of the mirror system, securing the mirror system to the wall of the oatmeal box.

6. After glue has set, pack the mirror system to hold it in place.

7. Sit the other clear circle on top of the mirror system and apply several dots of silicone to connect the clear circle to the side wall of the box.

8. Add goodies and snap the lid into place. If you don't have a lid, cut a clear plastic circle to fit on the end.

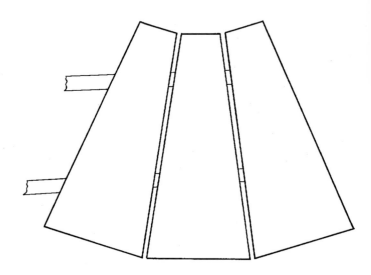

Hint:

This scope has a large, thin object chamber, perfect for long, skinny things. We decorated the outside with newspaper comics and used long thin strips of comics for the objects.

Also try thin twigs, feathers, leaves, or strips of film.

Variants:

This scope has enough room for multiple mirror systems.

Macaroni Chandala

Sherry Moser invented the "Chandala", a type of kaleidoscope which now exists in virtually every scope collection on the planet. She has graciously allowed us to take liberties with this wonderful design. What we have come up with has amazed even us.

We started to use a box that normally contains carmel corn and peanuts, (you know, the one with the prize), but we ended up with a standard macaroni and cheese box. After the prototype was built we found the 3 of us (with many years of scope experience between us) staring into a macaroni and cheese box for about an hour or more. Further, everyone who looks into this scope relates to it in some way, it is a very powerful and wonderful scope. You'll be eating lots of macaroni and cheese.

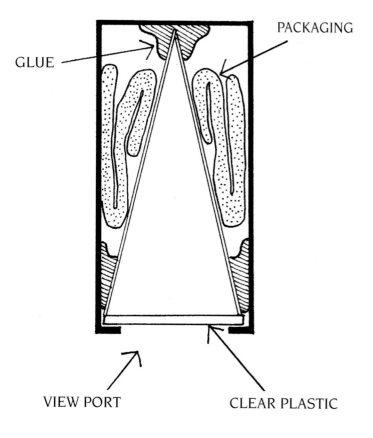

GLUE

PACKAGING

VIEW PORT

CLEAR PLASTIC

Materials:

1 box about 7 1/8" x 3 1/2" x 1 3/8", (macaroni and cheese box)

2 Pieces Front Surface Mirror 7" x 3 1/4" (it's worth the expense)

1 Strip clear .030 butyrate 1 1/4" x 7"

2 Strips clear .030 butyrate 1 1/4" x slightly less than 3 1/2"

Assembly:

1. Lay out the 2 pieces of front surface mirror face down on a non-scratching surface, along with the long strip of butyrate, and tape together.

2. Carefully turn all three pieces over and remove protective coating from the front surface mirror (if it has a covering). Gently fold the system into a triangle. The long strip of butyrate will be the view port so you will need to tape it lengthwise instead of straight across. Try to get as little tape as possible in the viewing area.

3. Open the macaroni and cheese box, save the contents, and shake out any crumbs that may want to stick in the box. Tear off flaps on both ends of the box.

4. On the long thin side of the box (7 1/8" x 1 3/8"), cut out a rectangle slightly smaller than 7 1/8 x 1 3/8", leaving a slight lip to contain the mirror system.

5. Slide the mirror system into the box so that the view port and the cut out rectangle match up, and set the box on it's side, view port down.

6. Pack the mirror system gently but firmly along the length of the box on both sides of the mirror system. This will center up the mirror system.

7. You may want to put 2 dots of silicone or hot glue, both ends, on the wide part of the mirror system, connecting it to the box.

8. At this point, turn the box over and with plastic

Macaroni Chandala *continued*

tape, carefully tape the edge of the box to the plastic on the view port. Use as little tape as possible so you have more viewing area.

9. Take a test run with plastic beads. Wipe them off so they don't bring clutter and dust into the mirror system.

10. We recommend using oval rice beads, 8 mm and 6 mm plastic beads, and tri-beads as show in the photograph. Try different combinations until you find "the" one you like best.

Place the 2 smaller strips of butyrate on either end of the box and secure with plastic tape. You may want to add overlapping tape until you don't see the mirror edges.

If you look in the triangular side ports, 3-dimensional "Chandala" type images appear, and you can tilt the box to your eye or away. Either way, it's hours of entertainment.

Hat Variation:

Just when you are starting to enjoy watching other people tilt, shake, roll, and gyrate into funny postures while staring into a macaroni and cheese box, your imagination is already visualizing what people will do when they put on this hat! It now occurs to you that all the fun and entertainment of viewing a scope in not necessarily inside the scope itself.

Constructing this variation of the Macaroni Chandala is quite simple. Place the scope as far out on the brim of a long billed fishing hat as you can, so you can focus on the objects. Add levelers, if needed, to adjust the view port to eye level, glue in place with epoxy or silicone, and let sit. If you have trouble focusing, cut a panel out of a reading magnifier and secure in the view port. Enjoy!

Hint:

This scope works wonderfully by looking into the view port and moving the box from side to side. The beads will roll and hop scotch over one another. We thought about calling this scope the "Macro" scope, but ended up calling it the "banana" scope or "fruit" scope.

Macaroni Chandala

Plentiful Pie

One of the most interesting scopes in this book, you can change the angle of the 2 mirror system and see as many or as few of the "pie slices" of the image as you want.

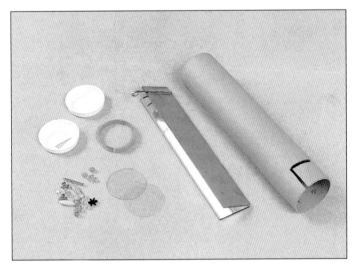

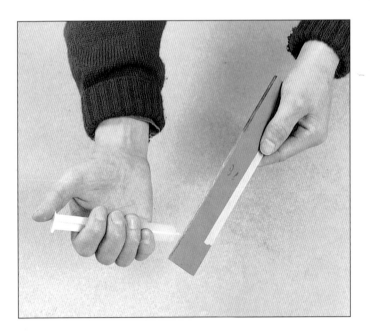

Materials:

Cardboard mailing tube, cut to 10" long and slightly
    larger than 2" in diameter
2 Plastic tube end caps
2 Strips mirror 8 7/8" long and 1 1/2" wide
2 Clear plastic disks .030 butyrate, slightly less than
    2" in diameter, to fit down into the tube
1 Piece of coat hanger wire 3" long
1 Cardboard spacer strip 3/8" wide and 6 1/4" long
    (If you have extra sections of mailing tube, cut
    the spacer from the tube and take out 1/4"
    of the ring.)

Assembly:

1. Clean the mirrors and put them together, reflective sides facing each other, and tape to hold in place. Run a small bead of silicone along one side of the long dimension. This will hold them together and let them

flex to open and close. Let sit for 2 hours.

2. At one end of the wire, with needle nose pliers, bend a loop 1/4" in diameter. This will get the cut end out of the way and provide a handle to open and close the mirror system.

3. Attach the wire to one end of the mirror system with silicone, a good thick coat to cover the wire completely. Let sit for 2 hours.

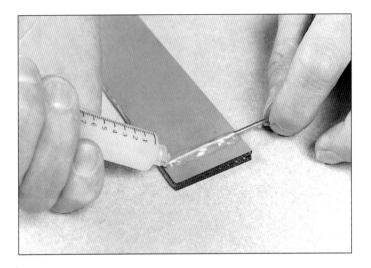

4. Cut a slot, 1/8" wide and 1 3/8" long, lengthwise in one end of the tube.

5. Plug in the end cap, along with one of the clear circles, in the other end of the tube and slide in the mir-

ror system (with the wire going into the slot). When the mirror system hits bottom you can guesstimate where to cut the opening for the wire to move back and forth to open and close the mirror system. This additional cut should be roughly 1 1/4". When you get your slots adjusted, slide the mirror system into the tube. The eye

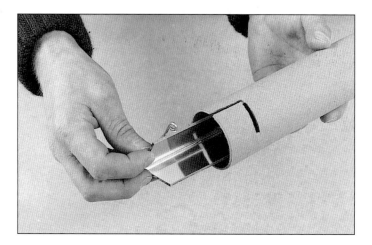

hole end cap is in the end of the tube.

6. With the mirror system closed, laying on the bottom of the tube, with the wire in the crook of the L, carefully attach two dots of silicone to the underside of the mirror system at both ends (carefully remove the end cap so the system doesn't move). This will attach

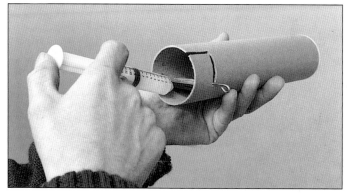

the bottom of the mirror system to the body of the tube. Let that sit for an hour or so. When set, pushing the lever should open and close the mirror system.

7. At the eye piece end, hold the scope up to the light and open the mirror system to half open and trace the opening for the eye hole. Cut the opening, replace the clear circle, align, and plug in the cap.

8. Place the other clear circle into the tube at the object chamber end, and dot with silicone in several places to hold in place. The mirror system should be able to open and close.

9. When the silicone is set, place the spacer ring in position and you are ready to load your goodies and put on the final end cap.

Hint:

This is a great study in symmetry. To get equal and exact replications the angle must be exact. Use the "stick trick" (see chapter on 2 mirror systems) to judge the equality and symmetry of the images.

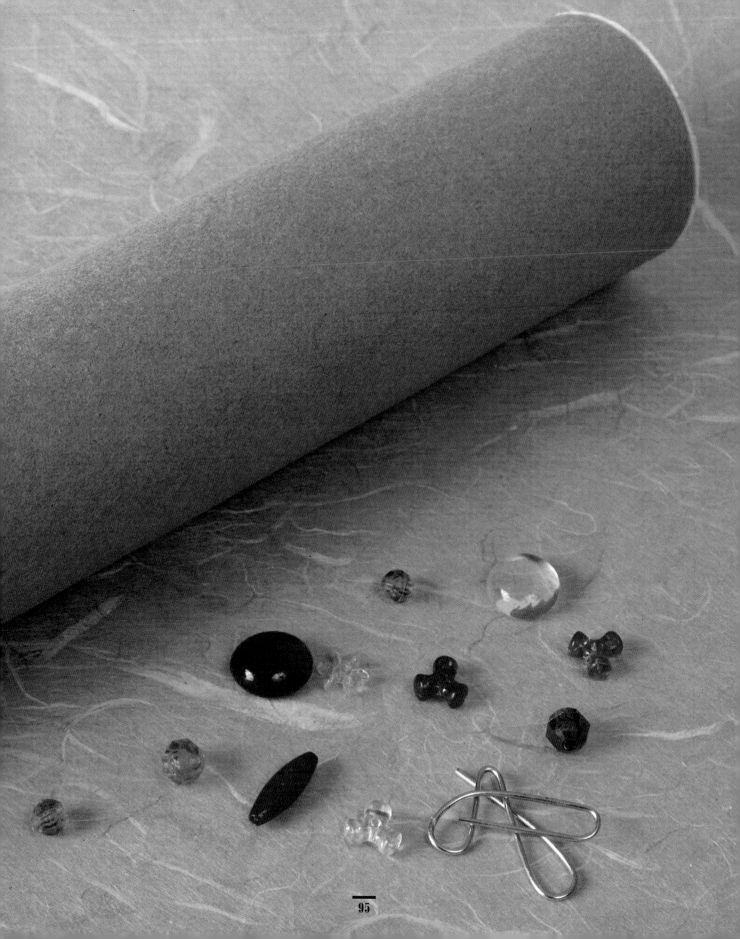

Rainbow Mailer

Polarized light, cellophane, clear styrene from CD cases, and cut up plastic cola bottles will amaze you with the vibrant colors they produce when viewed through a polarizing plastic sheet.

Materials:

US Post Office mailing tube with removable cardboard end 12"x2"

3 Strips mirror 11 7/8" x 1 3/8"

1 Clear plastic circle 2 3/16" for eye-piece

1 Polarized plastic circle 2" in diameter, cut from sheet

1 Polarized plastic circle 2 3/16" in diameter, cut from sheet

Cardboard spacer strip 1/4" to 3/8" wide by 6 1/2"long

Masking tape

Colored electrical or plastic tape

1/8" sheet styrofoam or other material for packing mirror system

Object chamber goodies:

1/2"x3/8" plastic cut from the screw-on neck of a clear plastic cola bottle

1 1/2"x1 1/2" (plus or minus) irregularly shaped clear styrene from broken CD or tape case

1 1/2 "x1 1/2" crumpled cellophane from an envelope with a window

Assembly:

1. With a hacksaw, neatlty cut off the metal ends on both ends of the tube. One of these ends is the one that slides off the tube while the other is fixed to the tube itself.

2. Assemble mirror system into an equilateral tri-angle type of system. Wrap in sheet styrofoam and secure mirror system in the tube, or use other packing material to secure the mirror system from moving. At this point the mirrors should be flush with both ends of the tube.

3. For the eyepiece end, use the tube end that does not slide off. Place the clear circle on top of the tube and tape in place with the colored tape. You may wish to tape over the clear disk until you have covered the exposed edges of the mirror system. Also, any nicks in the paper finish can be covered with the colored plastic tape.

4. Turn the tube over, take the smaller polarized plastic circle and spot with silicone around the edge of the tube. Place the disk on top and let set for an hour or so until firm.

5. At the end of the tube, where you put the first polarized circle, take 3/4" masking tape and make 2 laps around the end of the tube, right below the polarized circle.

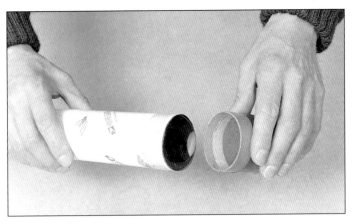

To make the moveable end of the kaleidoscope, you need to put masking tape on the outside of the main tube and on the inside of the small tube that fits over the main tube. To put a strip of tape on the inside of the end tube that slides off the main tube, wrap the mask-

ing tape backwards on your index finger several times and unroll the tape on the inside of the small tube about 1/4" into the tube. Smooth both tapes down with your finger so they can slide over one another and create the moveable end.

6. Slide the end tube over the main tube. You will feel tightness as the two strips of tape pass over one another. Slide on until the two tapes pass each other and you feel the tightness ease and the end tube will turn easily. If you look into this end of the tube you will see the polarized circle and have an end chamber of roughly 1/4" to 3/8" in depth.

7. Cut a strip of cardboard to the depth of your end chamber and 6 1/2" long, fold it into a circle and insert into the end chamber. This cardboard spacer will keep the moveable end from shifting down on the objects and pinching their tumbling action.

8. Load the cellophane, styrene piece, and the part of the plastic cola bottle neck. 9. Temporarily tape the 2 3/16" polarized lens on the end and take it for a test drive. Experiment with different types of plastics, styrenes, and cellophanes to get the colors you like, then use the colored plastic tape to secure the end lens to the moveable end of the kaleidoscope.

Bug Face

This scope utilizes the simplest mirror system: 1 mirror. Front surface mirror is not necessary to get great images. When long skinny objects are used, the images resemble bug faces.

Materials:

1 Cardboard tube 12" long by 2 1/4" in diameter with a 1/8" wall thickness

4 Circles .030 butyrate 2 1/4" in diameter (trace around the diameter of the tube)

3 Piece of brass strip 3/4" wide by 2" long and about 1/32" thick

1 Strip mirror 11 5/16" x 1 15/16"

Assembly:

1. With a hacksaw cut 1 /2" cardboard ring from the end of the tube. This will be the wheel or cell. Take 2 of the 2 1/4" clear circles and tape them temporarily to both ends of the 1/2" section.

2. Cut 3 pieces brass strip 2" long with tin snips. With pliers or vise, bend the last 1/8" of the 3 brass strips to 90 degrees.

3. Take the mirror and insert it in the tube. Center up the mirror in the tube and secure with hot glue or silicone to the back side of the mirror using two dots of glue connecting the mirror to the tube, on both ends.

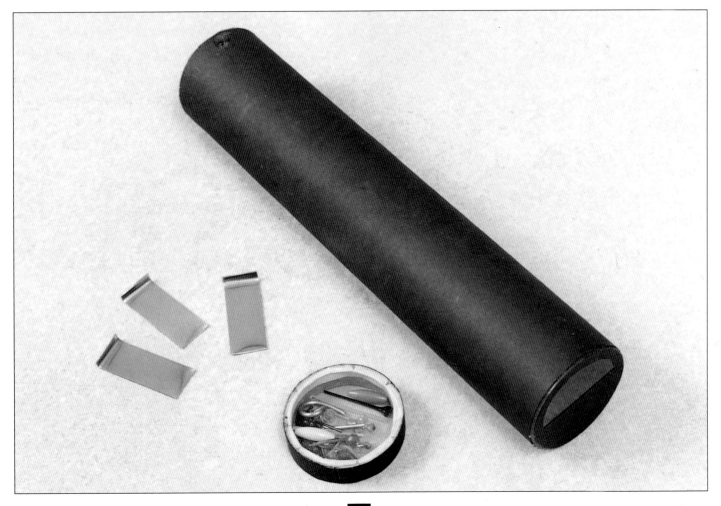

7. Take the final clear circle and scratch with fine sandpaper to prevent you from seeing straight through, or you could use a white plastic circle.

8. Prepare your mix for the end cell. Long skinny colored pieces along with bent wire tend to make good bug faces. Try one of your mixes, taped temporarily, and adjust as you like it.

9. Stand the scope body on its end, eye piece down, and place the cell on top of the tube. Using silicone, glue the 3 brass strips into position to hold the cell on the end of the tube (see diagram) and let silicone set.

Variants:

This scope can be made made into a model where you can change end cells. You may find several mixes that you really like a lot and want to save. In that case you can make a separate cell for each. If you do this, you may want to drill holes in the brass strips and use small screws to secure the strips, allowing you to change cells as you wish.

4. Glue a clear disk on each end of the tube with silicone, thus sealing the tube from dust.

5. Cut a circle 2 1/4" in diameter and cut out a large semi-circular hole for the viewing area. (*See diagrams*) Line up the eye piece with the mirror system and glue into place.

6. Take the 1/2" slice of tube and glue 1 of the clear circles onto an end.

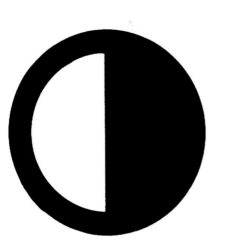

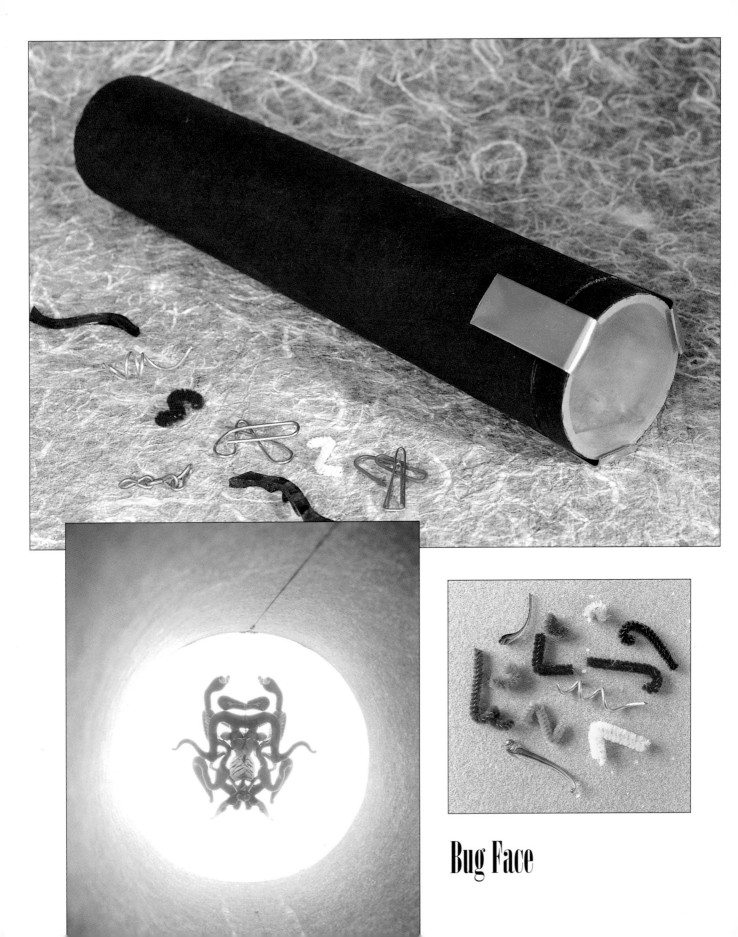

Bug Face

Marble-ous Chorus Line

If you have lost your marbles, go find them right now! And while you're out, look for a toothbrush box without plastic windows. (Thanks to Corky Weeks for her "chorus line" inspiration.)

Materials:

1 All cardboard toothbrush box 7 1/2" long
2 Strips .030 clear butyrate 5/8" x 6 1/2" long
2 Strips black cardboard 7/8" x 6 1/2" long
1 7/8" Cats eye marble, hopefully with 2 or 3
  colors in the center
1 Clear plastic rectangle to cover mirror system
  on the eye piece end

Assembly:

1. Open both ends of the toothbrush box. For the eye piece end, keep the flap, on the other end remove the flaps.

2. Assemble the mirror system in a square format. The clear butyrate will act as a mirror inside the dark box. Lay out the mirrors and cardboard in a "mirror, cardboard, mirror, cardboard" arrangement, fold up and tape together. Slide the mirror system into the box. With the mirror system flush with the eye piece end, close the flap and guesstimate where to cut a small hole (a hole punch might work well) so you can see inside the mirror system without seeing the edges of the

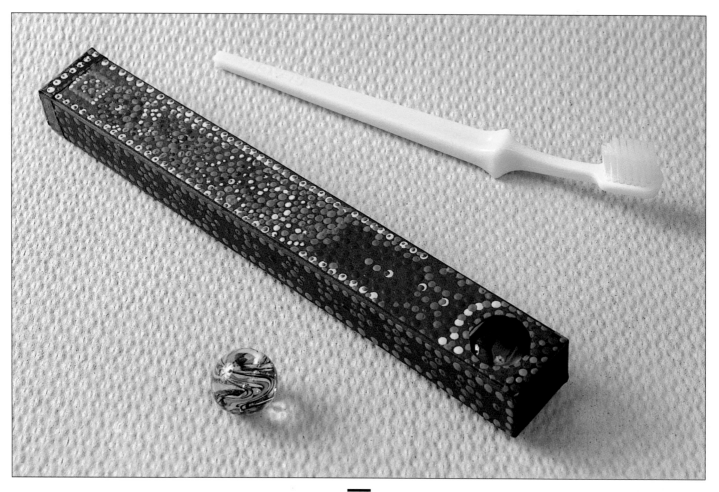

Marble-ous Chorus Line *continued*

mirror. Remove mirror system from the box.

3. At the other end of the box and about 1/4" in from the end, cut 2 round holes about 5/8" in diameter in the wider sides of the box. These openings will hold the marble in place and allow light to shine into the marble as well as giving you a means to turn the marble easily.

4. Slide the mirror system into place, flush with the eye piece end of the box, allowing a bit of room for the clear plastic rectangle to cover the mirror system at the eye piece end. Put 2 spots of hot glue or silicone to secure the system to the box.

Back to the other end, reach in and put 2 spots of hot glue or silicone to secure the system. Take care not to let the glue into the viewing area.

5. Push the marble into the end of the box, and away you go!

Go find any other marbles that you may have missed in your first search.

Tubular Brass

The very simplest kaleidoscope. Brass tubes purchased at hobby and model shops generally have a shiny interior surface, making a great continuously spiralling image when objects or colors are looked at through the tube.

Materials:

1 Thin brass tube 5/8" in diameter and any
    length beyond 8"
1/2" Cats eye marble

Assembly:

Put the marble in the tube and, with needle nose pliers, slightly bend the tube inward in 4 places at the end of the tube. Do this on both ends of the tube. This prevents the marble from rolling out of the tube. You may want to buff off any sharp edges or burrs on the end of the tube. You may want to wrap a soft collar around the ends of the tube, extending 1/4" past the ends of the tube, to protect the eye.

Look in one end and let the marble roll back and forth. Amazing.

Variants:

Use the tube as a teleidoscope, all by itself.

Put smaller marbles or plastic beads in tube to roll back and forth. Cover the ends with clear plastic and a soft collar to protect the eye.

See photo on page 104.

Plumber's Fantasy

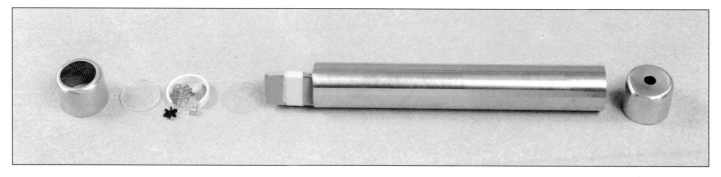

This is a classic scope, durable and beautiful, that's bound to be a coffee table hit. What a fantastic reincarnation of plumbing parts!

Materials:

1 9" x 1 1/4" length of the lightest weight hard copper tube you can get. DWV (Drainage, Waste, and Vent) if you can get it.

2 1 1/4" copper end caps

3 Strips mirror 7/8" x 8 1/2"

1 Clear plastic square 7/8"x7/8"

1 Clear plastic disk slightly under 1 1/4" or less, depending on wall thickness of the tube

1 Frosty or textured disk slightly less than 1 1/4"

1 strip of cardboard 3/8" wide by 3 7/8" long

Assembly:

1. In one end cap drill a hole 3/8" in diameter in the center of the end cap. You may need to deburr with a file.

2. In the other end cap drill a hole 1 1/8". This can be done with a hole saw, or you can have a machine shop "turn" these holes for you.

3. If your copper tube has been cut with an abrasive saw or a pipe cutter you will need to deburr the edges with a file.

4. Slide the end cap with the 3/8" hole onto the tube. If the cap fits loosely, a light tap with a hammer on the side wall of the cap will slightly oval it and make it fit tighter.

5. Drop the clear square into the tube, shake until it settles over the eye hole.

6. Assemble mirror system into an equilateral triangle format, carefully slide into tube and pack the mirror system to keep it from moving.

7. Insert the clear disk so that it sits on top of the mirror system.

8. Form the cardboard spacer into a circle and put into the tube.

9. Add goodies.

10. To close off the end, place the frosty disk on top of the tube and slide the end cap with the large hole over the tube.

Hint:

When removing end caps that fit tightly, remove with a twisting motion to prevent a sudden release, which creates a wonderful airborne rainbow crescent of flying goodies which are hard to locate on the floor. People with bare feet are sure to find any goodies you missed, much to their dismay. The twist-off plastic caps on a 1 liter plastic soft drink containers fit very well as end caps on this project.

Variants:

3/4" Tube 6" long with caps makes a pocket model kaleidoscope.

Tubular Brass

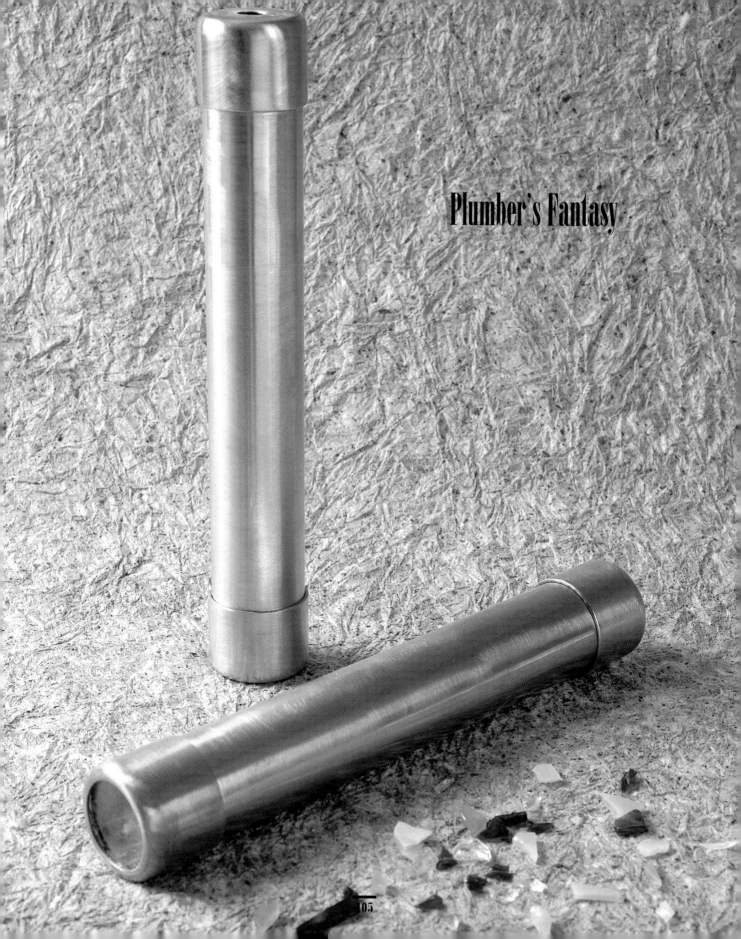

Plumber's Fantasy

Bamboozle

Nature's own kaleidoscope body is too good to ignore.

Materials:

1 length of bamboo, hopefully having died a
   natural death and having turned light yellow
   in color and very dry

3 Strips double strength mirror, cut to less than
   7/8" by 11 5/8"

.030 clear butyrate for the eye piece and a circle,
   size to be determined

Note: Since bamboo can vary greatly in size and shape, we will demonstrate our project on this particular size of bamboo and show you how to make alterations for your particular size of bamboo.

Assembly:

Bamboo stalks grow in natural sections. The sections are identified by raised rings that tell you where each individual section begins and ends. Within each section is a hollow tube closed off on both ends at the raised rings. Ideal sizes of bamboo are 7" to 12" long and 1 1/2" to 2 1/2" in outside diameter.

1. Select the section you want to use and, with a hacksaw, cut through the middle of the raised ring. This will leave a cut end that is solid, which will be the eyepiece end. At the other end of the section, cut just in front of the raised ring. This should give you a completely open end.

2. With a drill on the solid end, create an eye hole 1/4" to 3/8" in the center of the bamboo.

3. Clean out the tube to remove wood drillings and another matter that may be in the tube.

4. Measure or guesstimate the smallest inside diameter in the section. In our section the inside diameter was 1 1/4". Taking that figure and multiplying by .68, we got a figure of .85 of an inch, which is close to 7/8 of an inch. Just to be safe we cut the mirrors slightly under 7/8" to ensure that they fit in the bamboo section. Next, measure the inside depth of the section. Ours was 12 1/8" deep. To get the length for the mirrors, subtract 1/2" from 12 1/8" to get 11 5/8", which allows room for the clear eyepiece and the object chamber and the other disks. To make a complicated story simple the result was: less than 7/8" by 11 5/8" mirrors, cut 3.

5 Clean mirrors and assemble into an equilateral triangle format.

6. Cut a 1" square of .030 butyrate and drop into the tube, it should lay flat against the eye hole. Insert mirrors into the tube and pack so the system does not move in the tube.

7. Guesstimate the diameter of the tube and cut a .030 butyrate circle to fit on top of the mirror system and fairly closely to the sides of the tube.

8. Measure the remaining distance and cut a strip of

cardboard or other spacer material to fit down in the tube and be flush with the top of the tube.

9. Cut a disk of butyrate to match the end of the bamboo. Scratch the surface of the butyrate disk with fine sand paper to diffuse the light.

10. Add goodies and, when satisfied, seal butyrate to the end of the tube with silicone.

Hint:

This is a natural scope so you may want to experiment with dried flower petals, dried leaves, wood chips, twigs, or insect wings.

PVC-oozy

Of all the end chambers, the liquid filled ones give you the most peaceful and flowing images. A simple turn of the scope body sets the color in motion. Sit back and relax.

Materials:

1 9" PVC tube 1 1/2" with as thin a wall thickness
   as you can get.
2 mirrors cut to 1 "x 8 3/8"
1 Black card cut to 1" x 8 3/8"
2 Clear disks which will fit inside the tube
1 Plastic disk the same size as the outside
   diameter of the tube, preferably white plastic
   that you can't see through
Silicone and 12 cc syringe
Small bottle of glycerin

Assembly:

1. Cut the PVC tube to 9". Steel wool and alcohol will remove the printing on the tube.

Variants:

Bamboo can be scraped, producing color differentials on the barrel.

It can be coated with shellac or urethane to preserve the color and make a shiny surface.

If you have wood burning equipment, all kinds of decorations are possible.

You might want to change the goodies in the end. In that case you might use small screws instead of silicone to secure the butyrate to the end of the tube.

See photo on page 108.

2. From another piece of PVC cut a 3/8" wide ring off the end of the tube. With a pair of cutting pliers cut a 3/8" section out of the PVC ring. This will be the spacer in the object chamber.

3. Assemble mirrors in the 2 mirror format with the angle that you like. Slide the mirror system into the tube and stand upright.

4. Place a clear disk on top of the mirror system.

5. Load a small portion, 3 or 4 cc of silicone into the syringe. Practice squirting the silicone where you want it to go on something other than your scope. Watch out for stringers as you pull the syringe away from the application.

6. Reload the syringe, hold the clear disk down with a non-scratching stick of some type and carefully squirt a bead of silicone around the edges of the disk so that the silicone forms a seal all the way around the edge of the tube, sealing the disk to the tube. After you have run the bead around, take the point of a pencil and carefully run

continued on page 110

Bamboozle

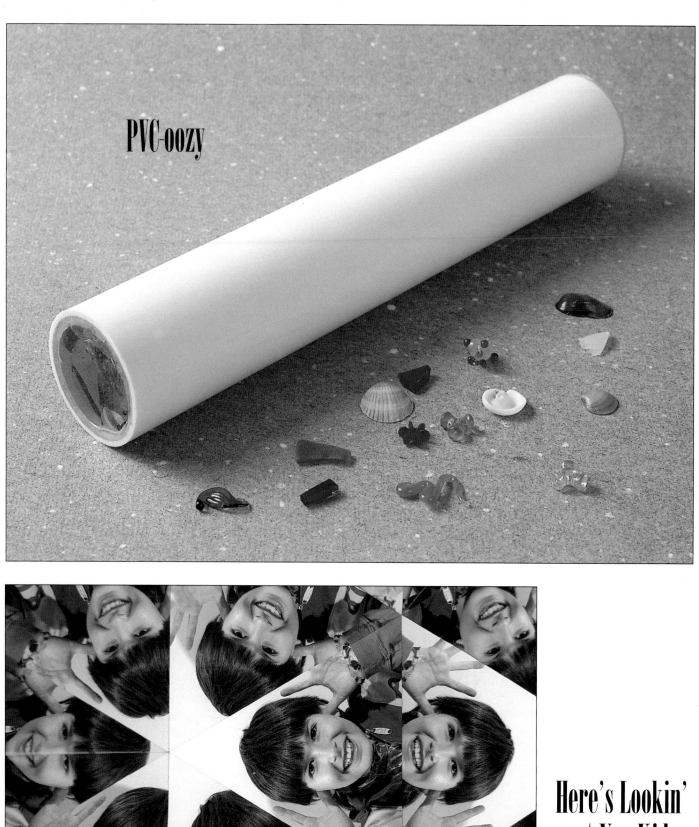

PVC-oozy

Here's Lookin'
at You Kid

back through the bead to make sure that there is contact all the way around and there are no gaps in the seal. Let sit for 24 hours (worth the wait).

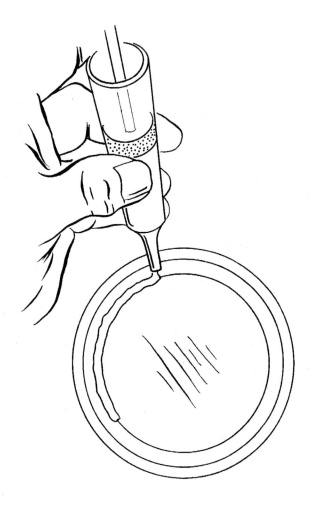

7. 24 Hours later, squeeze the spacer ring closed and push down into the tube. It probably won't go all the way down to the disk because of the bead of silicone, but that's OK. To check for fit, place the second disk into the tube so it sits on the spacer ring. At this point we want the final disk to be slightly below the level of the tube (this allows room for a thick bead of silicone to seal the fluid in). If necessary move the spacer ring up or down to accomplish this. When finished, remove the clear disk.

8. Load your goodies into the object chamber. It would be wise to have had some experience in what and how much stuff to put in the end chamber. As a very general rule you should fill the chamber about half full. Remember, glass sinks and plastic beads tend to float.

9. Load the glycerin into an eye dropper. Slowly add glycerin right into the middle of the chamber until it gets close to the top of the spacer ring. Leave 1/16" of the top of the spacer ring free of glycerin. Take care to make sure that no stray glycerin lands on the tube wall where the silicone seal is going to be, since any contact with glycerin will not allow the seal to work properly.

10. Place the clear disk on top of the spacer ring, load your syringe with silicone and run a bead around the edge of the disk to seal the disk to the tube wall. Go back with pencil point if you have doubts about the seal. Let sit 24 hours.

11. 24 Hours later, gently pack the mirror system to prevent movement. Hold the scope up to a strong light, put the eye piece disk up to the scope and mark the position for the eye hole, then cut the hole. This eye hole will be off center because this mirror system is a 2 mirror system.

12. Take silicone and dot around the edge of the tube, then place the eye piece in position on the tube and wait 1 hour to dry.

Thanks for your patience, it's worth it.

Variants:

3 mirror system
Seashells in object chamber

Here's Lookin' at You Kid

In this scope, we become the objects. The viewing area is on each end of the mirror system, and the system is large enough to reflect your whole face. Absolutely worth the time and expense. This scope will provide hours and hours of entertainment for people of all ages.

Instructions:

3 Mirrors, 4 feet x 12 to 15 inches wide, are assembled in a triangular format and secured with 3 to 5 wraps of duct tape.

Mirror must be at least 1/8" mirror (for strength and durability), or you might use mirrored acrylic sheet for the ultimate in safety.

You may also want to build a wooden cover that will secure the mirror system from breakage. Cover each viewing end completely with clear, unbreakable polycarbonate.

Set this scope on a table and let the fun begin.

Kaleidoscopic Photography

Pictures can be taken through this size of mirror system. If you use a flash inside the mirror system, you may need to dampen the flash with a piece of paper to prevent washout. With an instant camera you can adjust the flash with a few tries. Remove the clear polycarbonate on the camera end if it interferes with the flash.

Duck-in Play Scope

This standing kaleidoscope is sure to be a hit with the kids. Duck in and pop up in kaleidoscope land.

Instructions:

3 Mirrors, 6 feet long x 3 feet wide, are assembled into an equilateral triangle format, except the mirrors come together on the short ends instead of the long ends.

The size of this type of system can vary quite a bit. The longer the mirrors, the more people can be inside at one time. The height of the legs can be adjusted for the size people that are ducking in.

This type of kaleidoscope should be built with acrylic mirror for safety. As with any unit that is made for numbers of people to use, the emphasis should always be on safety and durability. If regular mirror is all you have, cover it with an unbreakable clear covering like a poly carbonate of at least 1/4" in thickness. Each mirror should be secured to a backing board, at least 1/2" thick plywood, with all the exposed mirror edges covered with mouldings. You may want to leave the mouldings off the short ends to get a good tight fit in the corners where the mirrors come together. Each individual panel should be built separately, then fastened together with the legs added on site. It travels better this way too.

Variants:

You could array this scope as a square or diamond system, which would allow more space in the kaleidoscope. Also you could use a chorus line system, perhaps leaving the ends off so people could walk through the mirrors on either side of them.

Index

Metric Equivalency	
Inches	CM
1/8	0.3
1/4	0.6
3/8	1.0
1/2	1.3
5/8	1.6
3/4	1.9
7/8	2.2
1	2.5
1-1/4	3.2
1-1/2	3.8
1-3/4	4.4
2	5.1
2-1/2	6.4
3	7.6
3-1/2	8.9
4	10.2
4-1/2	11.4
5	12.7
6	15.2
7	17.8
8	20.3
9	22.9
10	25.4
11	27.9
12	30.5
13	33.0
14	35.6
15	38.1
16	40.6
17	43.2
18	45.7
19	48.3
20	50.8